Personal Finance for Women

101 Must-Know Financial Literacy Tips

to Get Rid of Debt,

Repair Your Credit,

and Create Financial Independence

DLINA J.

Kindle Direct Publishing

Published By Kindle Direct Publishing

Kindle Direct Publishing is a division of Amazon.com

Paperback edition published 2023

Printed in the United States of America

DEDICATION

I dedicate this book to the memory of a beautiful, lovely, and honest person. My mom! "Adelina Da Rosa Goncalves and all of the hard-working moms!!!

Contents

Dedication 3

Acknowledgments 9

Introduction 10

1–The Psychology of Money 15

Money Worship 17

Money Status 18

Money Avoider 19

Money Vigilant 19

Unhealthy Money Fears and Self-Limiting Mindsets .. 20

Finance Myths That Hold Women Back 23

Developing A Positive Mindset, ... 26

Tips For a Positive Mindset 28

Identify Financial Goals 33

How To Set S.M.A.R.T Financial Goals? 34

Adopting an Abundance

Mindset Instead of a Scarcity Mindset 36

2—The Best Way to Bank 41

How To Choose a Bank 41

Modes Of Payment 45

Debit Cards 48

Cash Or Credit: Which One Should You Use? 49

3—All About the Benjamins 53

Savings 53

It gives You a Piece of Mind 54

Access To Funds for Unexpected Opportunities
and Unforeseen Or Unfortunate Events 54

Limits Debt 54

Increases Financial Security in Old Age 54

Financial Freedom 55

Saving Strategies 55

Budgeting 64

Budgeting Myths 66

How To Establish a Budget 67

A General Guide on How to Budget 69

Setting Up an Emergency Fund 72

When Should I Use My Emergency Fund? 73

How To Build an Emergency Fund 75

Budget Planner 77

4–Bang for Your Buck 79

Opportunity Cost 79

Spending Money Wisely 80

Track Your Spending Habits 81

Identify Areas to Reduce or Eliminate Spending 82

Understand The Difference Between
Wants and Needs 84

Apply Smart Shopping Practices to Save Money 85

Spending Freeze Challenge 89

5–Break the Bank 91

Debt 91

Low Income or Underemployment 91

Divorce And Relationship Breakdown 92

Poor Money Management 92

High Costs of Living 92

Overuse Of Credit Cards 92

Declining Health and Medical Expenses 92

Unexpected Expenses 93

Job Loss 93

Living Beyond Your Means 93

Education And Student Debt 93

Having Children 93

Failed Business and Business Expenses 94

Good Vs Bad Debt..94

 Ways To Avoid Debt 94

Strategies For Paying Off Debt Quickly 95

Credit...98

Types Of Credit...100

Establishing Good Credit..101

Repairing Bad Credit 103

6—FLOAT A LOAN 107

Loans 107

Student Loans 108

Managing Student Loans 108

Auto Loans..110

Car Financing Vs Car Leasing....................................112

How To Get an Auto Loan?..113

Mortgage 114

Buying Vs Renting: Pros and Cons 115

Basics Of Mortgage..117

Steps On How to Get A Mortgage...............................119

Summary Box: 122

Top Tips for Mortgage Shopping................................122

7—SITTING ON A GOLDMINE 125

Basics Of Investment..125

What Is Your Investment Style? 126

Types Of Investment 127

Inflation And Your Portfolio 132

4 Strategies to Mitigate Risk During
Volatile Economic Times 133

8—At a Premium 137

Insurance 137

Premium 137

Policy Limit 138

Deductible 138

What Kind of Insurance Do You Need? 138

7 Tips for Choosing the
Right Insurance Company For You 143

9—On The House 147

Benefits Of Starting Them Young 148

Four Principles to Begin Teaching
Financial Literacy 150

7 Tips for Teaching Your Child To Save Money 154

Conclusion 161

References 163

Dasneves Depina Biography 182

ACKNOWLEDGMENTS

First I would like to thank God because without God I would not have been able to accomplish anything in my life. Thank you, Mom and Dad, for all the dedication and hard work you did to raise me and to make me the person I am today. Thank you to my children for the love and encouragement that you have bestowed upon me. Thanks, husband, for being there when I wanted to give up, but you kept pushing me toward my goals.

I want to thank pa.publishing.com and all the team for the opportunity to engage me into an author's career.

Thank you for be part of this journey

Juwaiah Zia

Sharise Johnson-Moore

Shema

I want to thank everyone who encouraged me, motivated and inspired me throughout my life, and saw the best in me.

INTRODUCTION

"Too many people spend money they haven't earned to buy things they don't want, to impress people they don't like.
– Will Rogers.

My family struggled financially while I was growing up, even though my parents worked hard to provide for our household, so I rarely had new things. There is one memory that is vivid to me. My friend and I were hanging out at the mall. I passed a beautiful dress in the display window and remembered gazing at it longingly and imagining how beautiful I would look in it. It wasn't something my family could afford because it cost hundreds of dollars. It was heartbreaking to realize I couldn't afford it even if I spent everything I had, so while walking away, I vowed that I would never allow myself to feel this way again.

In my early twenties, I became financially independent, and a whole new world opened up to me. This pushed me to start splurging on clothes, shoes, and cosmetics. My salary alone was not enough to give me the things I thought I "deserved," though. I gathered credit cards to enable my shopping habits. I maxed them out but only paid the minimum amount due, and as time went by, my spending habits worsened. I spent hours scrolling online, looking at all the new, trendy things celebrities and influencers wore so I could add them to my cart. I ignored my high credit card balances and the insufficient funds in my savings. Whenever I felt anxious, stressed, or felt any other emotions come up, I would soothe myself by splurging. Until eventually, I was forced to see the truth.

After a particularly grueling month at work, I allowed myself to be persuaded into getting a pair of luxury designer shoes that amounted to one-third of my salary – even though I had convinced myself that I was only going into the store to look around. I justified it by telling myself it was a reward for working so hard. I was riding an emotional high while carrying the designer-labeled paper bag out of the store.

I stopped by the grocery store to pick up a few necessities. I even went in with the bag just to continue feeling the jubilation. As the cashier was punching up my items, I daydreamed of all the outfits I'd wear with the gorgeous new pair of shoes. I handed the cashier my card automatically when my total was rung up. Her words jarred me out of the trance I was in.

"Sorry, ma'am, but your card was declined. Do you have another one you can use?"

I handed over another card only to hear, "I'm sorry, this one's not working either."

My face got hot because I knew my third card was completely maxed out. I had no cash on me, either. I had to walk out of the grocery store without food, carrying the bag with the shoes that no longer brought me delight. I sat in my car and cried.

This was my wake-up call.

The need for change was only more apparent when I sat surrounded by the bills and statements highlighting how far into debt I had sunk. I felt helpless and insecure, trapped by the shackles of my current financial situation. My choices were limited, and it felt like I had given away the reins that controlled my life. Months passed, and I was no closer to knowing how to get myself out of this pit.

For a time, shame, and embarrassment about my lack of financial knowledge had me avoiding looking too closely at my bank and credit card statements. Feelings of fear, uncertainty, and worry plagued my every waking moment. I also avoided speaking to professionals about the financial issues that occupied my mind because they seemed too difficult to comprehend. But my lack of proactivity meant I was more vulnerable to exploitation by unscrupulous lenders and brokers who took advantage of my financial illiteracy for their benefit. It also meant I should have taken advantage of lucrative opportunities to lower my debt, save, and make money.

Do you understand the pain I felt? The powerlessness? The despair? Do you understand what it is like to lie awake at night feeling fearful about your financial future and worrying about not being able to provide for yourself or others who depend on you? Perhaps you are living paycheck to paycheck, with a large amount of debt, and without any savings or investments. Maybe you are stuck in a cycle of never having enough money and constantly relying on credit cards or loans to make ends meet. Maybe you are tired of being taken advantage of because you do not know enough personal finance to make sound decisions. You could hesitate to make investments because of a paralyzing fear of taking risks.

If you feel even the minutest stirring of affirmation to any of these questions or situations, I am here to tell you that you are not alone. Millions of other women around the globe struggle with similar issues, but there is hope for all of us.

You can live debt-free without relying on anyone else's income to sustain the kind of lifestyle you want to live. You can afford the things you want without worrying about where your next paycheck will come from or feeling guilty about spending on yourself and still having financial security.

I can say this with certainty because even though I had been living paycheck to paycheck, I completely turned my situation around and gained the financial literacy that granted me my financial freedom. My mission is to help as many women as possible conquer their finances, get out of debt, organize their assets, and achieve financial freedom the same way I did.

Money in the bank is more than just the number of zeros you accumulate. It's about the autonomy and security they grant us. Money is a means to gain independence. That liberty comes from gaining clarity of your financial situation and using tools and strategies to effectively take charge of your finances, and this book helps you accomplish those ultimate goals.

I do not promise a miracle cure for your financial woes. After all, it took me years to learn to budget, wise spending habits, how to invest with confidence, and more. But I can promise you will gain these skills faster than I did because you have the knowledge and experience to fall back on. the tips and strategies into action.

Picture a better future for yourself—one where you achieve your dreams and have control over your life without worrying about money. One where you have enough funds to live comfortably, have savings set aside for retirement and can indulge in luxuries smartly. One where you make ends meet even if something unexpected, like a medical emergency or when losing your job, happens. One where you have greater control over your destiny and can live on your terms. You can make this into your reality. Instead of just getting by, you can thrive. You can learn to use your money as a tool for creating positive change both in your own life and in the lives of others.

If you are ready to turn that possibility into your reality, turn the page.

1–THE PSYCHOLOGY OF MONEY

Let's be honest, money is a major part of everyone's life, and whether we would like to admit it or not, we are always thinking about it. We even alter our lives and choose professions that guarantee us more money because it guarantees financial security. But because having more money is so ingrained in us, we suffer from a lot of financial anxiety, and this is exactly why this chapter will tackle the beliefs, mindsets, and myths surrounding money. So, by the end, you will be able to understand your relationship with money and develop a positive connection with it. And with this, the famous words of Warren Buffett come to mind, "I will tell you the secret to getting rich on Wall Street. You try to be greedy when others are fearful. And you try to be fearful when others are greedy."

Understanding Your Relationship with Money

Everyone has a unique relationship with money. This relationship is a huge contributing factor to almost all major life choices, like your career, and even influences your spending habits. Your relationship with money also affects how you approach spending, saving, investing, and earning money. So having a healthy relationship with money means you will positively correlate with money and have a much easier time understanding how money works. You can ultimately use that money to maintain good health, invest the money in various ventures, and live a life free from stress and financial insecurity (Brown, 2022). Like my other things, our perspectives and subconscious beliefs or views regarding money are instilled in us when we are just children, and our habits often reflect our parents. Do you remember your parents either lavishly spending money, upgrading their stuff whenever they received raises, or do you remember your parents being particularly stingy with money, even if they had a lot of it? Either of these situations can create unhealthy spending habits in children. However, there is no need to worry; beliefs and habits can be modified, changed, or adjusted over time (A Healthy Attitude Toward Money Leads to Financial Security, 2019).

Tip #1:

The first thing you need to do is acknowledge your current beliefs about money before you can modify them. This may be uncomfortable initially, but this is essential in changing these old habits and developing new perspectives on money. Start by writing down the stories you tell yourself about money, what kind of language you use around money, and how you feel when you think about it. Once you have identified the negative beliefs, reflect on why they formed in the first place—perhaps from childhood experiences or messages from friends and family.

People with unhealthy habits typically fall under two categories: optimism and abundance or scarcity and pessimism. People who hold the latter view see money as a source of fear and anxiety and believe money should be accumulated instead of spent. These people also believe that no money will be enough, and often they don't think they deserve it. These people are fundamentally jealous of others and think the system is at fault for whatever financial failure or difficulty they might face. Surrounded by this negativity, people often fail to take action and miss many opportunities, making them spiral even more.

On the other hand, people who positively view money use it as a tool to reach financial success rather than thinking of it as an end goal. They are goal-oriented and have very stable and long-term goals. They spend less, save more, and even plan for the future or any unexpected expenses. The second type of people are much more successful and don't hold on to money as a lifeline; they know that money is an ongoing process, and its amount will continue to fluctuate throughout their lifetime. However, an excess of either of these habits can adversely impact children. (A Healthy Attitude Toward Money Leads to Financial Security, 2019).

We have already touched on that money problems stem from childhood, but how exactly are they perpetuated and sustained within our psyche? Well, the majority of these foundational beliefs we have regarding money act on a level that is unknown to us, which is why we often see examples of people who win tons of money but end up losing it within a couple of months and return to the original economic status within the society. Their foundational beliefs pushed them to make choices that didn't support their financial well-being in the long term. Aside from that, trauma is also a major contributing factor to how you view money. These traumatic moments don't have to be necessarily life-changing; however, these micro-traumas have an impact. If you were bullied for the quality and brand of your clothing as a child, you would hyper-focus on your clothes as an adult to protect yourself from being shamed and embarrassed again (The 3 Things That Create Your Money Beliefs, 2021).

Now that we are all caught up on why and how our beliefs are formed, let's move on to the four major beliefs linked to destructive and damaging money-related behaviors.

Money Worship

These people think money is the key to all happiness, so they love to surround themselves with it and flaunt it. At the same time, these people think they will never have enough money, so they often overwork themselves to reach that unhealthy money goal. Money worshipers are often compulsive spenders, have a major work-life imbalance, and are hoarders (Marter, 2021) (Spann, 2018).

> ## Tip #2:
>
> Achieving financial freedom isn't just about having more money – it's also about changing your mindset to focus on the things that bring you joy. Learn to prioritize experiences and relationships over material possessions. Rather than buying something, look for ways to connect with people or explore new places or activities. If you focus on building meaningful connections and experiences, you will ultimately find much deeper fulfillment and long-term happiness than just having money can bring.

Money Status

People who lead their lives by this belief system tend to define their self-worth by their net worth and how much money they have accumulated. They place great importance on buying the best and the most popular items because money signifies success. These people also pretend to have more money than they do, so they overspend. People like these are financially dependent, compulsive, and even spend secretly (Marter, 2021) (Spann, 2018).

> ## Tip #3:
>
> To stop believing that money is a sign of success and worth, it's important to remember that true happiness and success come from within. Instead of trying to make more money, focus on building meaningful relationships, pursuing passions and hobbies, and developing a strong sense of self-worth. Financial freedom can be important in helping you achieve these goals, but only if pursued for the right reasons and with a purposeful mindset.

Money Avoider

People who are money avoiders think of money as the root of all evil and tend to have negative or fearful responses. These people often think that they don't deserve their own hard-earned money. Despite being scared about money, money avoiders know that money will improve their lives and raise them to a higher status. These people have difficulty establishing financial goals and sticking to a set budget (Marter, 2021) (Spann, 2018).

Tip #4:

Re-frame your thoughts about money. The next step is replacing those unhealthy beliefs with more positive messages. For example, if you believe that "rich people are greedy and selfish," challenge that thought by reminding yourself that there are many ways to be successful financially besides taking advantage of others—like hard work and smart investments.

Money Vigilant

People with the vigilant personality type often hyper-focus on being frugal and constantly worry about insufficient savings. They are more stable and tend to focus on their financial security; however, vigilant people can hoard money to an unhealthy degree. Not having enough money is a huge source of anxiety for them that plagues their every waking moment (Marter, 2021) (Spann, 2018).

> **Tip #5:**
>
> Begin reading books or listening to podcasts on personal finance and success stories from other women who have achieved financial independence; hearing these inspirational tales will help replace any lingering doubts with self-affirmation and ambition.

Unhealthy Money Fears and Self-Limiting Mindsets

We all have our beliefs regarding money, and often these beliefs are a defensive mechanism that our mind has created to protect us from the outside world. The problem with these beliefs is that they are outdated and no longer relevant, they might have been when our belief was set in place, but they don't matter anymore. However, removing or changing them isn't easy because they are embedded in our subconscious minds. These beliefs lead us to subconsciously sabotage ourselves and keep us from achieving anything. This is why you need to recognize these limiting self-beliefs to pinpoint them in your psyche and understand how they negatively impact your life (Sabrina, n.d.) (Fox, n.d.). Here are some self-limiting mindsets and beliefs.

Believing That Money Is Scarce,

The scarcity mindset perpetuates the mentality that wealth and opportunity are limited and only some people can access them. People with this mindset think they will never have enough money and often become obsessed with what they lack. This mindset creates a tunnel vision for achieving specific financial goals that are either unrealistic or completely unachievable. The scarcity mindset has become even more common because of the pandemic since people lost their jobs. Unless they completely shift the way their business functions and move to the current demands of the consumers, the businesses will fail to sustain themselves (Yale, 2022).

However, this mindset can easily be shifted to look at the more positive aspect of achieving financial success by making small but daily changes to view and look at things. First, you need to focus on the abundance of money around you. You could even keep a list of financial wins for each day. The scarcity approach to the world comes from a hostile place, so try to force yourself to think of the opposite of your fears. While this may not be easy, if practiced daily, you will see a shift in perspective (Yale, 2022).

Money Doesn't Buy Happiness

Most of us have grown up with the phrase "money doesn't buy you happiness," so much so that we subconsciously start believing it. However, is it true? We need to understand what the phrase means in the first place. The phrase came around to tell people that while money can buy you houses, fancy cars, vacations, and all the things you will even want in your life, it doesn't buy you lasting happiness and joy. This phrase was coined by the rich, for the rich because they don't have to worry about basic human necessities like food, clean water, and having a roof over their head. While it is true that money doesn't mean that people will suddenly love you and be genuine to you, it is also true that these things aren't as important when you are struggling to keep a roof over your head. Money doesn't guarantee happiness or peace of mind, but for people who don't know when they will have food on the table, money certainly can buy them happiness (Mantilla, n.d.).

"The Rich Get Richer, And the Poor Become Poorer"

The "rich get richer, and the poor get poorer" might seem like a harmless belief, but it can perpetuate a lot of bitterness, disdain, and defeatism in people. People with this view, especially if they aren't financially well off or stable, might think of rich people as greedy, privileged, and bad overall. These simple messages might seem fleeting at first, but they affect us subconsciously and make us think that money is a scarce commodity and only for other people (Suzannah, n.d.)

Fear Of Not Having Enough Money

Many of us fear that we will not have enough money. While most of the time, these fears are entirely warranted; for example, you might be scared of losing your job or have experienced a devastating financial loss due to a bad investment. But for some people, this fear of "not having enough money" isn't brought on by significant investment; it's thought that it accompanies them everywhere they go and affects every decision they make. You might want to take a vacation because you have worked hard for it and deserve it, but you can't because you constantly worry about losing your job, even if it is impossible. While this fear isn't completely unfounded since we live in a time where your success is measured by how much money and monetary value you have, it becomes a problem when your fear takes the wheel and guides your every decision. You will never experience anything you want to because you fear the big "if." There is always more to do and more to have, and if you fail, look for resources around you because I assure you, you have them. You have jobs, as unappealing as they might be, and you have people and family you can fall back on, so look, hold on to that as a crutch if you have to (Kate, n.d.).

Fear Of Losing the Money You Have

We have experienced a lot of economic instability over the last few years, so losing money is quite a real fear. Still, when this fear stops you from spending on necessities and seeking health care services because you don't want to spend money, it becomes a problem. Some people who struggle with this mindset stop themselves from even thinking about their unhealthy spending or saving habits, and it often stops people from continuing what they previously enjoyed doing. People constantly check their bank and wallet to see how much money they have, and the thought of spending money or not having enough causes them to have anxiety and panic attacks (Hakeenah, 2021).

Finance Myths That Hold Women Back

Women have started climbing the social and economic ladder in the 21st century. However, the battle is far from over because even though women are just as successful as men, people still believe that men are better at managing finances than women. So, what unfounded beliefs lead to people underestimating women or women underestimating themselves? Let's discuss some of them (Money myths: 5 stereotypes about women and finances that we need to bust right now, 2018).

Women Must Be Dependent on Their Husbands for Financial Support

It is true that traditionally women stayed at home to take care of the kids while men went outside to find ways to provide for their families. However, women have grown outside these traditional boundaries of what it means to be a woman and have certainly become capable of providing for themselves. Women that exist in today's time don't need to depend on a man, or anyone for that matter, to sustain themselves. Rather, most families follow a double income structure where both parties earn money and divide the cost of living. But despite earning the same amount as their partner or sometimes earning even more than their partner, women are rarely involved in the financial planning for their future. This is often not because the women aren't interested or capable but because this mentality that women will always depend on their husbands is ingrained in us since we are young (Money myths: 5 stereotypes about women and finances that we need to bust right now, 2018).

Women Are Not Good at Managing Money and Investing Wisely

The idea that women are bad at managing money is a damaging stereotype set in place when we are young. The stereotype is perpetuated in every tv show or movie we watch, so we almost start believing it and self-sabotaging ourselves. To get out of this spiraling dilemma, women need to start investing in a financial diary to see how much and where they spend and not down all the spending despite being big and small. It can help you track where you spend the most money and reduce costs. And while it isn't as easy as it sounds, it will start taking effect if practiced long enough. (Money myths: 5 stereotypes about women and finances that we need to bust right now, 2018).

Women Can't Comprehend the Complexity of Personal Finance

While it is true that understanding math, stocks, credit scores, and inflations is difficult, women are more than competent enough to deal with these topics. Having the mindset that women aren't capable of doing something is what makes mathematics a male-oriented subject and restricts women from succeeding or even entering the field. Women aren't educated regarding these topics, so they can't understand how to manage their finances even if they want to. People need to be educated about handling money in their teenage years so they can make intelligent investing decisions as they grow up (Money myths: 5 stereotypes about women and finances that we need to bust right now, 2018).

Tip #6:

Seek out financial education: for someone who isn't taught how to take care of their finances, the language used in finance can be confusing and overwhelming for anyone. Seeking out personal finance education is key to developing a positive money mindset because it gives you the knowledge and confidence necessary to make sound financial decisions. Start by reading books written by experienced professionals and taking online courses from reputable sources that offer reliable information on managing money effectively.

Financial Matters Are Man's Duties; Women's Duties Are Restricted To Domestic Spaces

We have already discussed that traditionally women have taken up domestic roles while men took up roles that helped them earn money and provide for their families. But now, because women have also started earning money since the household cannot function unless the man is earning insane amounts, women are still expected to "pick up the slack" and take care of household duties while working full-time. But it is not right to assign roles based on a person's gender. Duties should focus on what chores a person is the best at, and they should be divided between the partners since both are earning money. Women will always be just as capable as men, so they must stop undermining their abilities. (Money myths: 5 stereotypes about women and finances that we need to bust right now, 2018)

Women Are Emotional and Impulsive

Buying something impulsively doesn't necessarily mean you have no self-control. If you don't fall outside your budget's parameters, your impulsive shopping won't significantly affect your financial situation. The next issue people have is that women are "emotional," so they shouldn't be allowed to handle the money since emotional people don't make good decisions. And while women might face important financial decisions brought on by an emotional and devastating life event, their emotions might not necessarily carry on to that financial decision. Women are more likely to ask people for financial advice if they feel lost or unable to make decisions, and because they are more risk-averse, they are less likely to invest in risky stock situations and incur a loss (Duke, 2010).

> **Tip #7:**
>
> Celebrate your financial success when you can. As a woman, you are constantly exposed to these damaging stereotypes and myths that make you feel you aren't worth enough. So, before building a positive money mindset, it's important to pinpoint your financial strengths and celebrate them. This could include having a steady job or income, having a small emergency fund, or simply making progress toward a financial goal. Taking the time to acknowledge your successes and progress will provide the motivation needed to tackle more difficult money challenges ahead.

Developing A Positive Mindset,

We have already established multiple times that we all have different relationships with money. How much our moods and emotions affect our relationship also differentiates person to person. A few emotions might encourage us to act a certain way, which is precisely why some people don't act rationally regarding Ney (Hakeenah, 10 Common Money Fears and How to Overcome Them - Money Psychology, 2021). Let's look at some prominent emotions and how they affect us.

Guilt

is an emotion that can manifest in multiple ways, but the most prominent way it affects you is by encouraging you to make decisions that are outside your best interest. You could put yourself in a position to donate because you have been too much for your friends, family, or people within your inner circle. You could also be thrust into situations that trigger actions damaging your financial goals, and you don't realize what is happening until your guilt goes away and you are met with the consequences of your actions. Most of the time, guilt can make you function against your interest and make you introspective and trigger positive rethinking. The guilt could cause you to look at unnecessary expenditures and consider how you could budget going forward so that you don't experience it again (Hakeenah, How Fear, Guilt, Shame, and Envy Affect Your Financial Goals, 2021).

Fear

Fear is probably the most dangerous emotion concerning money because fear naturally gives rise to anxiety about losing your money and becoming bankrupt or fearing that you will never succeed and never have enough money. Fear can cripple your decision-making skills, and to conquer it, you must first acknowledge and then learn how to manage it. Seek professional help if you have to since there are some things we can't solve on our own (Hakeenah, How Fear, Guilt, Shame, and Envy Affect Your Financial Goals, 2021).

Shame

Shame is often the opposite of guilt because guilt originates from letting others take advantage of you at the cost of yourself. At the same time, shame comes from being unable to meet the financial standard you have set for yourself. When you feel shameful about something, you naturally want to do anything to avoid thinking about it, but that won't make the problem disappear. If you don't identify where this feeling originates, you will lose all the financial progress you might have made and constantly focus on the wrongs rather than the rights. You will need to put in a lot of effort to combat this feeling and might even have to plan how to spend your money down to the last cent. But even after that, you might not always reach the financial standard you set; learn to forgive yourself because shame will only ever hold you back (Hakeenah, How Fear, Guilt, Shame, and Envy Affect Your Financial Goals, 2021).

Anger

Anger is a common emotion that emerges when you make a sudden financial decision; however, anger is never helpful. Instead of focusing on the fact that you have spent a lot of money, focus on how to ensure a situation like this doesn't happen again. This might mean budgeting more or setting up an emergency fund so you never struggle with poorly managed finances again. If you have to, seek professional help because anger can push you to make bad investments (Hakeenah, How Fear, Guilt, Shame, and Envy Affect Your Financial Goals, 2021).

Envy

Social media has made it much easier to pry into other people's lives and be envious of them because they seem to be achieving far more than you, even if they aren't necessarily that impressive or special. It is natural to want to be successful without making much effort because that's what you see influencers doing online, but people fail to remember that the grass is always greener on the other side. Envy should demotivate you; instead, you should let it push you further and help you achieve your financial goals. This could mean investing, budgeting, and saving money to reach a financial goal. Instead of comparing yourself with others and surpassing them, consider how to live the best life within your budget (Hakeenah, How Fear, Guilt, Shame, and Envy Affect Your Financial Goals, 2021).

Tips For a Positive Mindset

If you want to start building a positive mindset, you need to focus on three key aspects: delayed gratification, building resilience, and not comparing yourself to others. Delayed gratification can be a huge tool to help us manage our finances and encourage our minds to think positively. Delayed gratification is when you delay the feeling of gratification and immediate reward in favor of a bigger or long-term reward. When we are children, we want immediate gratification, but as we grow into adulthood, we must temper our desire and consider the practicality of our purchase. You could use this method to put off purchasing something that you don't necessarily need so that you could save up the money and go on a vacation or have savings and financial independence. It might not be easy to employ delayed gratification in your life, so you need to start small and create goals that are much easier to reach, making them more difficult as time progresses. You should also make rules for spending money; for example, you could tell yourself that you can only spend money on yourself once you get paid or pay all the bills and budget for that month. Delayed gratification is so that you can reach a certain financial goal, so if you feel like you might flatter at any step, remind yourself of your goal (Importance Of Delayed Gratification, n.d.).

Tip #8:

Understand the importance of delayed gratification and find ways to implement it. If you can wait a moment to make a purchase, especially large or expensive purchases, you are much more likely to budget better and avoid unnecessary shame and debt.

We all face adversity during our lives, and we can't do anything to control it; all we can do is control our reaction to that situation. These external events, whether on a global or personal scale, take a huge toll on your health, mood, and overall outlook and can often leave you feeling overwhelmed and anxious. And, as I said, there is no way to escape adversity; all you can do is find ways to better your situation and regain that lost sense of control. Resilience can be hard because it isn't something we are born with. It's an active and ongoing process that requires you to make an effort. You need to face struggles so that you can build resilience, and you need to feel your emotions so that you can process them properly. Drowning your problems in drugs and alcohol and numbing yourself isn't the way to go. To build resilience, you must start by accepting that change is inevitable; things happen for a reason, while it may sound cliché. Thinking about it from a positive perspective might shift how you view the situation. Instead of focusing on what you can't control, focus on what you can and put active effort towards that. If things get hard, always remember to reach out to people. You are constantly surrounded by people who ask for help, whether from friends, family, or even professionals (Robinson, 2023).

Tip #9:

It might be difficult, but maintain a positive perspective during financial hardship or loss. Remind yourself of what matters, such as your family or health, which can help you stay motivated during hard times. Find constructive ways to channel energy and worry into action steps that could lead to progress so that you can slowly start feeling like there is hope for a better future. Ultimately, you can only remain hopeful about the future and take it one step at a time.

Most of our insecurities originate from comparing ourselves and our situation with others, especially influencers, on the internet. We are always under the unfortunate assumption that we will be happier if we buy the next thing, but seeking validation and completion from objects will never work because we will move on to the next best thing. Plus, wanting something because someone else has it is pretty silly because we all are different and unique, and that dress or that relationship that looks so good on the screen just might not be for you. Instead of comparing yourself to others and what they have, focus on what you are thankful for. Some people even benefit from a social media cleanse, which means deleting or logging out of their social media for a day or a week and just focusing on themselves (Loredo, 2022).

Tip #10:

Avoid comparing yourself financially with others or measuring success by material possessions. This comparison only leads to envy and feeling inadequate. Instead, measuring success based on individual progress and accomplishments is far more empowering. Nothing is wrong with wanting nice things, but material possessions never indicate true success. Focus on individual goals and building resilience in the face of adversity because they are worthwhile endeavors. Learning to appreciate accomplishments, regardless of financial or material gains, can lead to greater satisfaction and appreciation for all you have achieved. Focus on living within your means and enjoying life's experiences without overextending yourself financially.

Understand Your Financial Values

Making any decisions related to your money directly reflects your financial values. These values are external and internal reasons that determine how you feel about money, shaping your financial decisions. Money values impact your thinking and how you view and spend, so when your actions align with your financial values and your values reflect your goals, you lead a much more fulfilling life. To get on the right track with managing your finances, inspecting your financial values and making positive changes if needed (Perez, 2017). Here are some ways you can determine what your values are.

Create A List

Money is intertwined with our lives and impacts every part of it, so while trying to understand your financial values, you must write some financial goals you would like to achieve in each area of your life. You could form questions that envision what your future might look like five years down the line, and this will reveal a lot of things you don't even know about yourself and highlight what is important to you so that you can continue working towards that goal (Sabrina, Money Values: How To Align Your Priorities With Your Spending, n.d.).

Prioritize

Once you have figured out your goals, you need to sort them in order of importance so that you can allocate the appropriate amount of attention each financial goal needs. We have a limited income, and wanting to contribute to each aspect might put unnecessary financial pressure on you. By prioritizing the important goals, you distribute the money and time towards something that means a lot to you (Sabrina, Money Values: How To Align Your Priorities With Your Spending, n.d.).

Know Your "Why"

Identifying goals is more manageable, but to make them come true, you need to identify why they are essential to you.

While you might have plans to save money for a vacation, your motive could be to create everlasting memories and explore the world. So, the goal may seem simple at first, but a lot goes into making that goal special for you. Once you figure out "why" something is important, it will motivate you, even more, to contribute towards your goal and discourage you from seeking instant gratification (Sabrina, Money Values: How To Align Your Priorities With Your Spending, n.d.).

To help you get started, here is a list of common core money values:

- Being generous

- Establishing a sense of financial security

- Building relationships

- Creating a relaxing lifestyle

- Having more options

- Experiencing a fulling and improved life

- Giving your children more opportunities

- Having a piece of mind

- Reducing money-related anxiety

(Sabrina, Money Values: How To Align Your Priorities With Your Spending, n.d.)

> **Tip #11:**
>
> Always look at the bigger picture and ask yourself questions like "What do I want my money to say about me?" "What kind of legacy do I want to leave with my wealth?" This reflection type can help you develop strong core values for approaching finances.

Identify Financial Goals

Now that we are clear on financial values, we can move on to identifying financial goals that support those values. When I think about financial goals, this particular quote by John J Beckley comes to mind, "Most people don't plan to fail; they fail to plan." Identifying financial goals is necessary because it gives you a reason to save or spend money. These goals can be short-term or long-term, but either way, you will need to identify your goals first if you want to reach them. But why exactly is it essential to figure out your financial goals? Establishing financial objectives can help you shape your features for the better by helping you figure out the actions that will take you there. Identifying goals enables you to create a realistic and achievable plan to reach those goals and track your progress along the way. Setting financial goals is a lot easier than you think, and all you need to do is figure out what you want, make a realistic plan, and follow through with the steps. Although people who cannot practice delayed gratification might have difficulty looking at the bigger picture and establishing long-term goals. This is exactly why you need to learn S.M.A.R.T. financial goals (Schwahn, 2019).

How To Set S.M.A.R.T Financial Goals?

Smart is an acronym for Specific, Measurable, Attainable, Realistic, and Timely, and by creating S.M.A.R.T. goals, you will raise your chances of succeeding in those goals.

- Specific: You need to make sure that your goals are specific, so figure out how much and how you want to achieve that goal. This means figuring out how much money you need to reach a certain financial goal. Next, you need to know why you need to achieve that financial goal because you need a clear direction to start working toward that goal.

- Measurable: Your goals should be measurable because you can easily check them to see if you are making any progress.

- Attainable: Once you narrow down your goal, ask yourself if it is attainable and, if it isn't, how you can make the goal attainable. You are the only one who can decide if a certain goal is attainable because only you know how capable you are. Prepare not only for any obstacles you might face while achieving the goals but also prepare backup plans.

- Realistic: Aside from being attainable, your goals must also be realistic. This means that you need to set goals that you know you will be able to accomplish. Long-term goals can look quite unrealistic at first glance, but as long as you break them down into achievable steps, you can achieve them.

- Timely: Lastly, you must set a deadline for achieving your goals. Think about short-term and long-term deadlines and reflect each month to see how much progress you have made and whether you need to change or modify anything.

(Chan, 2020)

It might seem easy initially, but how exactly do you implement these in your goals? Well, consider you are saving for a down payment for a house, and you want to turn it into a S.M.A.R.T goal. You first need to make it specific, so your goal is to save just enough for a down payment for a house. Your measurable element will be the money you need, so just assume you want to save 30 thousand dollars for the down payment. The next thing to do is make that goal achievable. Thirty thousand dollars is a lot of money, so you want to set targets and save a certain amount each month. Your goal must also be realistic, so the amount you aim to save is achievable and realistic, depending on your monthly income and expenses. Finally, you must set a realistic time-frame for reaching the money goal (Lazar, 2022).

Tip #12:

Rather than basing your financial goal on other people, it is important to ensure the goals reflect YOUR individual wants and needs. You should consider what would make you content and fulfilled in the long term and then base your goals on that.

Tip #13:

Break down each goal into smaller achievable steps with deadlines attached so you can monitor the process. Setting intermediate milestones will help you stay motivated to reach your goal.

Adopting an Abundance Mindset Instead of a Scarcity Mindset

We have briefly touched on the scarcity mindset but didn't go into much detail about it and how to overcome it. People with a scarcity mindset believe they will never have enough money, so spending money triggers fear and anxiety and holds them back from experimenting and trying new things. This mindset naturally comes from a very negative place. It isn't healthy because people with a scarcity mindset live a sad life, constantly fearing that they will go into debt if they go outside the minimal budget they have set for themselves. This fear stays even if there is no possibility of that happening. Suppose you want to live a healthy and happy life and want to enjoy your money without fearing the worst. In that case, you need to make a conscious effort to move from a scarcity to an abundance mindset. Here are five ways to shift your perspective (Why Is Adopting an Abundance Mindset Important? 2021)

1. Focus on the things you have!

It is human nature to focus on the things you don't have and use that to discourage yourself from applying for a new job or picking up a new hobby. Instead of focusing on what you don't have, try reframing your perspective and thinking about how your current experience would help you apply for that new job and whether you enjoy that hobby. Not everything is quantifiable and provides monetary value, so as long as you enjoy it, continue doing that hobby, even if you aren't necessarily good at it (Castrillon, 2020).

2. Surround yourself with positive people!

Your company affects how you view the world, so if you are struggling with looking at the positives, surround yourself with people who will help you spot those positives. If your current friend group isn't enriching your life, it is time to make new friends (Castrillon, 2020).

> ### Tip #14:
>
> Connect with like-minded people who have similar financial goals since they can support, motivate, and inspire you to overcome financial obstacles. Many online communities exist today specifically designed for women looking to achieve financial independence – take advantage of these resources where you can find advice from other women like yourself who want to stay accountable during their quest for greater financial stability.

3. Create positive situations!

In most fights or disagreements, one party loses, and the other party wins, but it doesn't have to be that way. Try to think of ways to create a win-win situation and brainstorm until you find a satisfactory solution for all parties (Castrillon, 2020).

4. Practice gratitude.

If you want to improve your overall well-being, you must start practicing gratitude. It is challenging for negative emotions to take root when practicing gratitude for the things you have or achieved. One way to do this is by jotting down five things you are grateful for daily (Castrillon, 2020).

5. Train your mind to recognize opportunities.

With an abundance mindset, you can easily spot opportunities, resources, and choices. When you stop focusing on one thing, your brain can expand its reach and notice things you wouldn't have observed naturally (Castrillon, 2020).

Self-Limiting Beliefs	Empowering Beliefs
• I will never have enough money.	• There is a multitude of ways to make money.
• I am selfish for wanting money when there are so many people suffering.	• The money I earn can be used to help people.
• I will barely get by and struggle to live paycheck by paycheck.	• I have complete control over my money and can budget properly.
• I can't help my social status.	• I can create the life I want for myself.
• I am not good with money.	• I know how to handle my own money.

Summary

- The first step to living a financially stable lifestyle is finding out the kind of relationship you have with money.

- A lot of people grow up with self-limiting beliefs about money, which taint how they view money, and these fears stop people from experiencing and enjoying life.

- There are finance myths that mainly target women and hold them back from talking about and dealing with finances.

- Over time, women have proved themselves to be self-sufficient, and now, many of them have their own careers and businesses. If they are smart enough to own their own business, they are undoubtedly capable of taking care of their finances.

- Women must start their journey toward financial independence by developing a positive mindset regarding money and overcoming their fears.

- People building a positive mindset must focus on three main aspects: delayed gratification, not comparing themselves with others, and building resilience.

- Start by understanding your financial values and create a list of your goals and figure out which goals are essential to reaching them.

- Set S.M.A.R.T. financial goals. This means that all of your goals should be specific, measurable, attainable, realistic, and timely.

- Try to develop a more abundant mindset and avoid the scarcity mindset.

- To develop an abundance mindset, surround yourself with positive and driven people that add value to your life and share your goals.

2–THE BEST WAY TO BANK

A report published by the Bank Administration Institute or BAI pointed out that children often use the same bank as their parents. Reports showed that in 2021, more than half of the millennials use the same bank as their parents. This was a major change from the year before because more than 54 percent of millennials used the same institute as their parents in 2020. This change isn't just happening because some banks are losing relevance but because people are becoming more aware of the kinds of deals available. The advent of the internet has changed how people live. Millennials have that advantage which allows them to research the financial options available to them and pick out the deals that benefit them the most. This phenomenon has also motivated the banks to provide better products and services at a much more affordable price to keep the customers happy. But what exactly does a bank have to do with your financial decisions? Well, choosing the right bank is one of the biggest keys to financial success, and by understanding and exploring how banks work and the deals they offer, you can make sure that all the choices you are making regarding your finances are the correct ones.

Thinking about where to start can be quite overwhelming, which is exactly why this chapter will focus on the basics of banking, particularly how to choose a bank, the types of accounts available to you, and the best way to utilize payment modalities (Sorrentino, 2022).

How To Choose a Bank

All banks offer different services. Naturally, there are different charges, levels of services, and different types and percentages of interest provided on the money you store in the bank. This means that choosing the bank might be the essential decision, and you need to choose the right one for you and your needs.

There are three types of banks: traditional banks, online banks, and credit unions, all of which are different. Traditional banks are the most common and have been around the longest. They provide ATM services, allowing you to access your cash from any ATM of your choice. They also allow you to make deposits and pay bills online. If you prefer to do your banking in person, these traditional banks are the right choice. Online banks, on the other hand, don't have any physical branches, and because all the work is done online, they are much cheaper since they don't have to pay overhead charges. However, some people find it frustrating to communicate with employees online. Lastly, credit unions are a great alternative to traditional and online banks since they are member-owned and have lower fees and higher interest rates. However, most credit unions don't have features such as online banking, which can frustrate people (Khartit, 2022). Now that we have discussed different types of banking, let's move on to the steps you need to follow in choosing the right account for you.

1. Identity The Right Account

Choosing one service can be tricky, especially when banks offer many different products and services. However, a good place to begin would be to examine your financial goals and priorities and find accounts that match them. The most common accounts are checking accounts, savings accounts, money market accounts, and certificates of deposit (CDs) (Bennett, 2022).

If you want a checking account, you need to go to a traditional bank or choose a high-yield account offered by some online banks and credit unions. If you are looking for an account with a high return rate, consider opening a savings account. Online banks offer better return offers because of lower overhead costs, and they are just as safe and credible as traditional banks, granted that they are insured by the FDI. Money market accounts are very similar to checking accounts, but they allow you to write a check and even provide you with ATM and debit cards. Lastly, a certificate of deposit is one of the best ways to earn interest since you will earn a guaranteed rate of return in exchange for locking that money for a certain amount of time. However, you won't be able to use the money saved in the CDs until it matures, so if an emergency emerges, you might have to pay additional fees (Bennett, 2022).

2. Look For Banks That Charge Low or No Fees

Most of the time, you have to pay certain fees to access the services the bank offers. However, some banks don't require you to pay any fees or have deficient fees, and naturally, you should always choose banks with lower fees. Make sure you don't sign up with any banks that charge monthly maintenance fees, overdraft fees, or ATM fees. And if you can't find a bank without monthly maintenance fees, contact the bank and see how you can waive these fees (Bennett, 2022).

3. Consider The Convenience of Bank Branches

When you think about banking, one major concern is convenience, which is why you need to think deeply about ATM and branch locations and the availability of online and mobile banking services. Choosing which services you want depends on what you are accustomed to, so if you want the convenience of mobile banking, you will choose banks that prioritize those services (Bennett, 2022).

Tip #15:

Stay one step ahead of out-of-network fees by establishing an account at a bank with extensive ATM coverage. That way, you can always access your funds without worrying about costly surcharges.

---

4. Take A Look at Credit Unions

with higher returns and interest rates because they aren't typically made for tons of profit. They are local or regional and pride themselves on creating a personal connection with their customers, which is why they serve specific communities. This is exactly why the services provided by credit unions tend to be more personalized. People are generally discouraged from using credit unions because they seem less credible than traditional banks. However, credit unions are often backed by NCUS insurance, which ensures that the government backs your credit union, and your money will be safe, even if the union fails (Beers, 2022).

There are a few drawbacks to credit unions. First of all, credit unions are limited to regional or local areas, so they might not be available in your area so there is no point in using a credit union that might not even have branches in your area. Secondly, you can probably get even higher rates if you choose an online bank. Lastly, you might have to work a particular job or live in a certain area to be able to become a member (Beers, 2022).

5. Find A Bank That Supports Your Lifestyle

It is very common to get influenced by someone else and choose the bank they use; however, you always need to consider your lifestyle and then choose an account or bank that works with that lifestyle. You could even have separate accounts if you have a couple of goals, one for normal use and one for emergencies (Bennett, 2022).

> ### Tip #16:
>
> **Look for banks that offer services tailored for you- like budgeting tools or rewards programs. It may take some extra time, but it is definitely worth the effort since you find a financial partner who supports your needs.**

6. Examine Digital Features

Almost all banks have apps or websites now that allow you to transfer funds, check your balance, make cheque deposits, and even pay your bills. However, not all banks offer certain features like locking debit cards so thieves can't use your card information. If that is an important thing for you, choose a bank that can offer you these services. But always remember to compare banks and services and read customer reviews before settling for one (Bennett, 2022).

7. Understand The Terms and Conditions Read

Reading the terms and conditions can seem very tedious, but it is important to explore everything to ensure that you don't miss any hidden fees. If you are required to pay monthly fees, the terms and agreements might tell you ways you can waive them. Also, when you compare banks and their services, keep an eye out for promotional offers because they can expire (Bennett, 2022).

8. Reviews For Banks You Are Considering

We live in the digital age, which allows us to use resources like reviews and weigh the advantages and disadvantages of something before we invest in it. This saves us from many scams and unsavory deals, so you must read reviews before choosing a bank since you will be sticking with it for a long time (Bennett, 2022).

Modes Of Payment

Modes of payment basically refer to ways the funds are transferred from one bank account to the other. The modes of payment aren't limited to receiving or transferring money but can also include withdrawing cash for personal use, so there are a few ways you can use money: debit cards, credit cards, cash, and cheques.

Cash

Cash is one of the oldest forms of payment, and it is still used as a tool. There are many benefits of cash, but the most common one is that you have immediate access to funds. However, cash isn't the most secure way to make payments since it can be easily lost, misplaced, stolen, or even destroyed, and because cash doesn't leave a paper trail, you can't get your money back if you have been scammed (TFIG, n.d.).

Cheque

A cheque is a dated and signed way to direct a bank to pay a specific amount of money to another person. Cheques can be both deposited and cashed, so it is great for making monetary exchanges between parties. There are a few kinds of checks; let's discuss them.

- **Certified Cheque** - This kind of cheque is guaranteed not to bounce because it is certified that the giver has enough money.

- **Payroll Cheque** - This kind of cheque is given to an employee by an employer to compensate them for their work.

- **Cashier's Cheque** - This cheque is signed by a bank employee because the bank is responsible for the funds. Cashier's cheques are required for larger transactions like buying or mortgaging a house.

- **Bounced cheques** - These are bad cheques used when making large transactions, but they don't work because the payee has insufficient funds.

(Kagan, 2021)

The bank typically issues Credit Cards, allowing you to borrow funds from the bank. When the cardholder initiates a transaction, they agree to pay the money back to the institution within a limited period of time and also pay interest. There are several different types of credit cards (Cussen, 2022). Let's explore them.

Standard Cards

Most of the time, these cards don't have an annual fee, and they simply allow users to use a certain amount of credit.

Premium Cards

Premium cards have special privileges, such as allowing you access to high-end airport lounges, special events, and so much more. The only drawback is that they require you to pay a higher annual fee.

Reward Cards

These cards offer users some rewards based on how they use the card. These prices can include travel points and cash back.

Balance Transfer Cards

These cards have introductory rates and fees and allow you to transfer money to another credit card.

Secured Credit Cards

These credit cards require you to pay a deposit to the bank before utilizing them.

Charge Cards

These cards don't have a monthly limit, but you can't continue using the card if you don't clear up your bills for the month.

Credit cards have a lot of benefits. They allow you to build your credit history, which is often necessary to buy a house or a car or take out a mortgage.

They also provide you coverage if your warranty expires. Additionally, they protect you from card theft or fraud. However, there are quite a few disadvantages of credit cards. First, spending money without a limit can quickly put you in debt, especially if you spend above your means. Secondly, having a credit card and not using it or paying your bills late can severely impact your credit history. Lastly, there are quite a lot of fees you have to pay to keep the card functional, and these fees don't include your interest, which has to be paid separately for each purchase (Cussen, 2022).

> **Tip #17:**
>
> **Do you want to increase your vacation budget? Take advantage of credit card rewards! Utilizing a frequent flier program that allows you to earn airline miles is an efficient way to enjoy discounted flights and make the most out of your credit cards.**

Debit Cards

A debit card is similar to a credit card since it allows you to make payments; however, the biggest difference is that the money comes directly from the user's account rather than from an institution. There are three types of debit cards: standard, EBT, and prepaid.

- Standard Debit Cards- These cards draw directly from your bank account and use the money you already have.

- Electronic Benefits Transfer Cards- These cards are typically issued by the government and allow users to use the benefits to make certain purchases.

- Prepaid Debit Cards- These cards are filled with balance and allow the users to make electronic purchases up to the charged amount.

(Cussen, 2022)

Debit cards are great for people who don't have impulse control and are scared of overspending and going into debt. These cards don't have any annual fees, and they even protect you from fraud. Although, there are a few cons that might be a bead breaker for you if you consider choosing this payment mode. Debit cards don't have any rewards, nor do they help you build credit, so if these are some of the services you are looking for, consider choosing a credit card instead (Cussen, 2022).

Cash Or Credit: Which One Should You Use?

Deciding which mode of payment you will use is very important because it ultimately determines what account and bank you choose. Both cash and credit have their benefits and disadvantages, and in the end, choosing between them depends on what you are looking for. However, it might be a little difficult to understand where to get started, so let's make it easier for you to decide (*Cash Vs. Credit: Which to Use?*, 2021).

When To Use Cash

Cash is a very easy way to shop for things since it is available everywhere and convenient. Here are a few reasons you might want to choose cash over credit.

When You Want To Avoid Fees

Credit or debit cards require you to pay monthly maintenance fees, so if you want to minimize the amount of money you spend, it is a good idea to pay with cash (*Cash Vs. Credit: Which to Use?*, 2021).

When You Want To Keep Credit, Use Low

Credit scores have a huge impact on mortgages and loans, and according to the CFPB, if you want to have a good credit score, you should keep it below 30 percent. So, if you see your credit score exceeding that amount, try switching to cash to minimize the damage to your credit score (*Cash Vs. Credit: Which to Use?* 2021).

When It's More Convenient

Sometimes, it is just easier to use cash, especially if you are buying food from street vendors or tipping someone. So, if you are looking for convenience, use cash (*Cash Vs. Credit: Which to Use?* 2021).

When You are Having Trouble Staying On Budget,

Having a credit card can quickly get out of hand, and you can easily overspend. If you want to keep on budget or are having trouble sticking to one, try switching to cash (*Cash Vs. Credit: Which to Use?* 2021).

Tip #18:

Paying with cash is a great way to stay on budget. Withdraw the amount you plan on spending ahead of time, and then you will know exactly how much you can spend. This will decrease impulse buying and save you from a lot of finance-related headaches.

Tip #19:

if you don't want to lug around tons of money, you could always choose a debit card. They are an efficient way to budget since you can track your purchases with real-time updates. Plus, they come equipped with extra security features like fraud protection and zero liability policies in case a card is stolen or used without permission - so you can be sure that money transactions are secure every time.

When To Use Credit

Credit cards can be very beneficial if they are used correctly. Here are some reasons to choose credit cards over cash.

When You Want Something Back

Credit cards offer you a lot of rewards, and they can often give you travel points or cash back. If that is something you want, consider using a credit card (*Cash Vs. Credit: Which to Use?* 2021).

When You Want to Build Credit,

Credit cards help you build your credit scores. These scores can be very helpful in proving that you are a responsible applicant so that you get better deals and interest rates (*Cash Vs. Credit: Which to Use?* 2021).

When You Want to Feel in Control,

It is much easier to monitor money using credit cards; you can see exactly where it went and manage your expenses. You can also set up autopay and pay bills automatically without having to worry about missing the deadline (*Cash Vs. Credit: Which to Use?* 2021).

When You are Traveling

Credit cards make it so much easier for you to travel since you don't have to worry about misplacing your cash. Additionally, it has become much easier to scam people on the internet, and when you order things online, there is a high chance that you will not get the product you paid for. This is why it is a good idea to pay for these purchases with a credit or debit card because if something does happen, you can ask for a chargeback. You can also lock your card if you lose it or if it gets stolen, so you never need to worry about misplacing it(*Cash Vs. Credit: Which to Use?* 2021).

Summary

- Choosing a bank will be one of the most important decisions of your life since it can affect your financial situation so make sure to do your research and choose one that fits your goals.

- Checking accounts are great if you want the convenience of a debit or credit card, but if you want to save, you need to get a high-yield savings account.

- Choose banks that have low overhead fees so that you can save as much money as possible. If you are looking for especially low overhead fees, open an account in a credit union or an online bank.

- Always look for a bank account that supports your lifestyle.

- It may seem tedious but understand and read all the terms and conditions before signing with a bank.

- Think about the modes of payment before you settle for a bank account. Do you want the convenience of a credit and debit card, or do you prefer using cash? This is because banks charge money for cards, so there is no use signing up for a card and paying money if you have no interest in using them.

- Credit cards are great if you want to build your credit, but if you fear falling into credit card debt, use a debit card instead since it uses the money you already have in your account.

- If you want to avoid extra fees, avoid using cards and stick to cash.

3–ALL ABOUT THE BENJAMINS

Picasso stated, "Our goals can only be reached through a vehicle of a plan, in which we must fervently believe, and upon which we must vigorously act. There is no other route to success." This quote really puts into perspective why financial tools are necessary in order to reach your financial goals. Taking its importance into account, this chapter focuses on talking about saving and budgeting so that you can successfully put money aside and create a budget and an emergency fund.

Savings

Saving basically means putting aside a portion of your income for the future. But why exactly do we need to save money? Well, a lot of people have different goals for saving money, and these goals can be both long-term and short-term. For example, you could be saving a portion of your money to buy a new phone, or you could be saving to eventually buy your own home (What is Saving? n.d.).

It might seem confusing to some people why people wait to spend their money when they could simply buy whatever they want at that very moment. However, there are quite a few reasons why people don't just spend all their money on things they like all the time. First, not all people make the same amount of money; in fact, most people are working for minimum wage. In addition, some people don't just have the responsibility to look after themselves; most of the time, they care for a family member and even pets, so financial flexibility might not be easy for them. This might still not be enough to convince people who have never really saved money in their lives because they never needed to, so here are a few major benefits of saving (What is Saving? n.d.).

It gives You a Piece of Mind.

Knowing that you have a certain amount of money accumulated in the bank takes a huge burden off your shoulders. It ensures that you will be able to provide for yourself and others and will be able to handle any emergency expenses (Importance of Savings, n.d.)

Access To Funds for Unexpected Opportunities and Unforeseen Or Unfortunate Events

You never know when you might run into an unexpected situation, and most people never prepare for them, so when they do run into trouble, they don't have the mental capability nor the financial backing to take care of that problem. They might need to ask friends and family to help arrange for the emergency funds, and while depending on them is fine, it's not a good look, and it can even affect their financial situation (10 Important Benefits of Saving Money, 2019)

Limits Debt

Having savings can limit the amount of debt you might fall under since you won't have to rely on credit cards to buy things for yourself. In the beginning, credit cards seem very convenient; however, that is far from the case since you will buy things for the credit cards and then pay interest on your purchases, and if these bills aren't cleared, they continue to pile up until you are totally in debt. Having savings will also prevent you from taking out emergency loans, and these loans often have much higher interest rates (5 BENEFITS OF SAVING MONEY, n.d.).

Increases Financial Security in Old Age

Most people think of the short-term benefits of saving, and the majority of the time, they save because they have some sort of goal to reach; for example, some people save money so they can buy a car, property, a new phone, or fund a vacation. And while there is nothing wrong with saving for a short-term goal, saving can also have a lot of long-term benefits, and one of these benefits is saving money for retirement. Most people don't work jobs that give them retirement funds, so it is completely dependent on them to come up with ways to save money for their retirement. Even people who get a pension don't get enough to cover all their needs. Saving just a small percentage of your income over a period of several years can give you a substantial amount of money for your retirement. Most people don't want to save money for retirement because, to be honest, life is unpredictable, and you don't even know if you will live long enough to see those funds in action, but what if you do live? That question alone should motivate you to secure your feature comfort by spending just a little less today (10 Important Benefits of Saving Money, 2019).

Financial Freedom

When you have money saved up, you can freely use it without feeling guilty because you have accumulated the money to sustain your lifestyle. It is relaxing to know that you have finances to fall back on if urgent funds are needed. This is why there is a stark contrast between people who live from salary to salary and people who save their money and then spend it freely (10 Important Benefits of Saving Money, 2019).

Saving Strategies

Here are a few saving strategies that can make it easier for you to save money.

Pay Yourself First

"Pay yourself" has become a very popular phrase in personal finance, and it basically means giving yourself a certain amount of money, but really that money goes into a specific savings account. Since your money automatically goes into a savings account, you are technically paying yourself first, at least a future version of yourself that will thank you for making a dedicated contribution to the savings each month. While it doesn't necessarily sound exciting, thinking about paying yourself some portion of the money you have worked so hard to earn before giving it all away in bills makes that monthly contribution much more special and personal. It naturally removes the temptation to skip a month and splurge. You could decide how much you want to save on your own, and this usually depends on the reason you are saving the money and how much you can afford to save (Kagan, 2021)

Cut Back on Unnecessary Expenses

If you review your spending habits and then cut out smaller expenses like unsubscribing to unused services, you can probably save a lot of money. Here are some other ways you might be able to cut down on unnecessary expenses.

- After a long day of work, people don't really have the energy to cook food at home, which often leads them to order takeout. But ordering food every day is not only very bad for your health, but it can also make a major dent in your earnings. Even though it is tough, try making food at home at least twice a week. If cooking every day isn't realistic for you, then you can use your weekends to prepare meals for the week so that you have the majority of the work done and only have to heat up the food during the week. You can follow the same ideology for coffee. It is very convenient to grab a cup of coffee on your way to work but spending money on coffee every day or a couple of times a day may seem like a small expense, but it can add up to hundreds of dollars a month. So, try making your coffee at home so you can cut down on the cost of buying coffee daily.

- The best piece of advice I have ever been given is that you should never shop without a grocery list and on an empty stomach. When you go in without a plan, you are more tempted to buy something because you might need it. Making a list can help you stay on track; find the items you want much quicker and make meal planning and prepping much more affordable and organized.

- Sometimes, we subscribe to a service in the heat of the moment, use it a few times, and forget to unsubscribe. So, you basically end up paying for a service you are not using. It's time to unsubscribe and start saving that money or at least put it to good use.

- Set all your bills on autopay because when you are busy, it is easy to forget to pay the bills, which means having to pay additional late charges.

(54 Ways To Save The Money, n.d.) (Reiner, 2022)

Tip # 20:

Take time to think about each purchase before making it so that you know you aren't just buying it in the heat of the moment. Ask yourself: Is this something I need now? Will this purchase make me happier in the long run? How often will I use it? These questions can help avoid impulse buys that add up over time and distract you from reaching your financial goals.

Open High-Yield Savings Accounts with Online Banks

A high-yield savings account pays you about 20 to 25 times the typical savings account. Usually, people pick one bank and open a checking and savings account to easily transfer funds back and forth. However, online banks have drastically changed the banking industry by providing citizens access to internet-only banks that provide you higher saving rates, and because of this, other banks have also started to offer higher interest rates in the shape of "high-yield savings accounts." But the rates offered by traditional accounts and high-yield accounts can't be that different, right? Well, just consider that you open a savings account with 1000 dollars and save 100 dollars every month on top of that. A traditional savings account offers you a 007 percent interest on your savings, while a high-yield saving account offers 0.50 percent. After 12 months, a traditional bank will pay you 1.16 dollars, while a high yield will pay you 8.27 in interest. This value may seem small but just look at the difference in interest (Lake, 2023) (Karl, 2021).

There are a few disadvantages to having a high-yield savings account. First of all, you might need to use different institutions for your accounts, and while it isn't a big issue because you can easily transfer money electronically, it's just a small disadvantage to keep in mind. Additionally, institutions that offer high-yield savings accounts have limited features, so your institution might not offer ATMs, credit and debit cards, and checking accounts. So, in order to access your funds, you might have to open a checking account in another bank (Karl, 2021).

Tip # 21:

When looking for a high-yield savings account, finding one with competitive interest rates and limited fees is important. Make sure to compare the annual percentage yield (APY) of different banks and financial institutions, as this will determine how much you earn on your money over time. Additionally, look into any introductory offers or bonuses that may be available. These can help you maximize your earnings in the early stages of an account. However, remember to consider any possible fees or service charges associated with opening and managing the account.

Utilize Windfall Money Wisely

When you receive a windfall, more commonly called a bonus or money you receive outside of your regular income, your first instinct is to spend it. However, there are quite a few ways you can maximize this income, so let's discuss some.

- You first need to ask for advice because extra money can come with its own set of challenges. Consider reaching out to an attorney, a financial advisor or planner, or a tax professional to know how to manage your money since windfalls are tax refunds, lottery winnings, and lawsuit settlements.

- Although it isn't the most exciting thing to do, you should pay off all your pending debts as soon as you get a windfall. Doing this can free up money to reach other financial goals that might be pending and also improve your credit score.

- Set some money aside in your emergency fund for any unplanned future events. And if you haven't started an emergency fund, now is the great time to do so.

- After setting aside some money for an emergency fund, make a contribution towards your retirement fund.

- It is always a nice gesture to consider your friends and family when you receive a windfall; however, make sure that you aren't being overly generous and letting people take advantage of you.

(What to do with a sudden financial windfall, n.d.)

> ## Tip # 22:
>
> **Spending windfall money freely and quickly can be tempting. However, you need to resist the urge to splurge and instead use the extra funds strategically to build your future.**

Find Ways to Increase Savings

The cost of living is through the roof currently, and even people who were already working 9 to 5 jobs have started to work a second job to be able to support themselves. And even if you aren't struggling to get by, everyone can benefit from a side job since it can drastically make your life comfortable and help you reach your financial goals. Before you start the business, here are a few things you might want to consider.

1. Although a side hustle is a second priority, you will still be spending a lot of time on it, so before you invest money and effort into it, make sure that your schedule can support a second job.

2. Working more than 40 hours a week can be very overwhelming for people, and after a long day of work, most people don't really have the creativity or drive to undertake another project, that is, unless you are passionate about the project. A side hustle will demand a lot from you, so make sure that it is something you are enthusiastic about to motivate yourself.

3. We don't need to monetize every hobby or everything that brings us some sort of joy; however, if you are in debt or need extra money, a hobby or business you don't profit from might not work for you. In addition to that, side businesses aren't profitable right off the bat, and you might need to build your client base and credibility in the industry before you start getting orders or profits. This is exactly why you need to keep the initial cost low.

(Ferguson, 2020)

Now that we have touched on a few things that might affect your side business, let's discuss a few side hustle ideas.

- Create handmade goods- There is something special about hobbies turning into profitable businesses. Many big businesses started as small independent sellers that made products in their spare time. You could turn anything into a business, whether it's painting, crafting, crocheting, or even carpentry. Creating things by hand definitely takes a lot of time, and people can buy something similar for a lot less price from fast fashion companies, but handmade things are often one of a kind and are made ethically. Also, handmade things are rare, so it is a really easy way to stand out in an industry saturated with fast fashion. Being a smaller business, you have a lot more opportunities to align your practices with your ethical beliefs and contribute positively to the planet, which is why smaller businesses use recycled materials and eco-friendly packaging.

- Use social media and start influencing- With the advent of apps that let you short-form content like YouTube, Instagram, and Tik Tok, becoming famous and sharing your passion with the world has gotten a lot easier. Many people have started to leave their full-time jobs after getting famous on Tik Tok and have become full-time influencers, and there is no reason you can't either. You don't need to have a rare hobby to become famous; most people become famous by reviewing products. It will take time for you to start earning any money, but building a slow audience is much better than blowing up instantly because the latter seems to fade just as fast.

- Teach online courses- You can teach the skills and subjects that you already have to people around the world. If you have worked in multiple places, you can discuss how someone can pass an interview, how to negotiate salary, or even how to ask for a promotion. Many new graduates don't have information like this. They are looking for all the help they can get in this competitive industry. You can use platforms like Coursera and Udemy to reach an international audience or YouTube.

(Ferguson, 2020)

> ## Tip # 23:
>
> When selling used items online, it's important to do some research on what similar items have recently sold on the sites you're considering. This will help you price your item competitively to maximize your potential profits. Clearly explain its condition and provide accurate measurements and descriptions in order to maintain a positive reputation with buyers. Also, cleaning up your item and taking good photos will help it stand out from other similar items.

Leverage Compound Interest to Grow Your Savings Overtime

Compound interest is amazing because you are not only earning interest on your balance but your interest is reinvested, so you earn even more profit on it. If you want to grow your savings in a short time, compound interest is the way to go, especially if you have a high-yield savings account. Consider the example we discussed when we were discussing the difference between savings and high-yield savings accounts: you have an initial deposit of 1000 dollars and add 100 dollars every month. Suppose you have a high-yield savings account that gives you 0.50 dollars of profit. In that case, you will earn approximately about 8 dollars in 12 months. Still, if you add compound interest to that equation, your money will be reinvested into your savings account. You will earn interest on those 8 dollars as well. While this may not seem like a big difference, I mean, how exactly are 8 dollars going to change your life? But we have to think about the long-term sustainability of our accounts. Remember that we are living in a time where money is losing value fast, and if you keep your money in a high-yield savings account and compound interest, you will at least be able to keep up with the inflation. Not to mention, you will obviously grow your savings over time and will be earning interest and compound interest on that as well, so over a period of 5 years, you will earn a good chunk of money, obviously depending on how much you save. But before you go and start an account that compounds interest, you need to understand a few key variables.

- The first thing that impacts your compound interest is the interest rate that you earn on your deposits.

- The second thing you need to think about is how much money you are starting with. Compounding interest adds up, but it is based on your initial deposit.

- The compounding frequency also affects your interest since money can be compounded once a day, monthly, or yearly. This will determine how quickly your balance will grow.

- Your compounding interest depends on the duration of your savings account. The duration basically refers to the period of time you will own the account, and the longer you leave your money in the account, the more interest and compound it has.

- Lastly, you need to consider your monthly deposits and whether you will make any. Additionally, you must consider how often you will be making withdrawals since the pace used to build principal balance makes a huge difference in the long run.

(Ashford, 2022)

Once you understand these key aspects of compounding interest, you will be able to make a much more educated decision about it and will be able to ask appropriate questions.

> **Tip # 24:**
>
> Start investing as early as you can and consistently into accounts that are earning compound interest. Compound interest is an incredibly powerful tool to grow your savings over time. By leveraging the power of compound interest, you can make your money work for you and watch your savings grow exponentially over the years — taking advantage of the opportunity to earn interest on both the principal and previously earned interest. This can have a huge impact on how much money you have saved in retirement or for other long-term goals.

Budgeting

Saving can only work if it is done alongside budgeting, but what exactly is it? Budgeting is a detailed plan of how you plan to spend your monthly earnings and finances in general. This basically allows you to evaluate your earnings in advance and see whether you will have enough to cover all tour expenses. If you discover that you don't have enough money, then you can figure out a way to access extra finances, be it getting a part-time job or borrowing money, or even restructuring your budget to get the most out of it. Budgeting can be a very powerful tool because it allows you to fully control how, where, and when you spend your money. After you grasp the basics of budgets, you will be able to track your spending down to the very last penny. People are generally very surprised when they budget because they see how much money they are spending on unnecessary stuff. When buying something, you function with the "what damage could five dollars do to your finances" mentality. The problem with this is that you are spending a lot more than just five dollars each day, and those dollars can add up. Budgeting helps you spot these spending and control them so that you can stick to your financial plans and reach your goals (What is Budgeting? What is a Budget?, n.d.) (Caldwell, 2021)

The problem is that the word "budgeting" leaves a bad taste in people's mouths because they think that budgeting means you have to pinch pennies, make sacrifices, and make drastic cutbacks in your everyday life, and for most people, this is life-changing. But the budget doesn't necessarily have to be any of that. Most of the time, it helps us understand where we are losing money and allows us to see whether we will be able to afford our lifestyle for a month. It also allows us to cover our needs and still indulge without going into debt (What is Budgeting? What is a Budget?, n.d.) (Caldwell, 2021)

> ### Tip # 25:
>
> Take an inventory of all the money you have coming in and out of your household, such as income, rent/mortgage payments, credit card payments and any other regular outgoing funds. Having a thorough understanding of your income can help you determine if you are spending within or beyond your means. Try creating a budget spreadsheet that tracks all of your expenses every month on a customizable template based on the information you already know about yourself. This will give you an accurate picture of exactly how much money you are receiving and spending each month and make it easier for you to allocate funds accordingly.

Budgeting Myths

Some common budgeting myths stop people from fully utilizing it, so let's discuss some of them and debunk them.

You Have to Be Good with Numbers

While it is true that you need some basic math knowledge in order to make a budget, it by no means is a difficult thing to do. As long as you can do the basics of math, which are addition, subtraction, multiplication, and division, you will be able to do it easily. And if that seems a bit difficult for you, then you can utilize apps and calculators to do the math for you (Top Budgeting Myths, n.d.) (Ramsey Solutions, 2022)

I Don't Have Time to Budget

Once you figure out how to structure your budget, it will not take you a lot of time to set it up. There are plenty of apps and other budgeting tools you can look into to make the process even more seamless (Top Budgeting Myths, n.d.).

I Already Budget Because I Keep Track of Everything I Spend

Keeping track of all your spending is just one aspect of budgeting, so there is a lot more to budgeting. For one, budgeting is supposed to be a financial plan for the upcoming month in which you decide how much and on what you will spend the money. This can look different for everyone; some people start the budgeting process by layout all the bills and utilities and how much they will cost. Others focus on examining their spending from last month and factoring that into their budget (Ramsey Solutions, 2022).

Budgets Are Restrictive

People run away from budgeting because they assume that they have to say goodbye to everything they find pleasurable, and while budgeting works best if you have self-control and abstain from impulse buying, you don't necessarily kill your every wish. You might have to give up spending money on a few smaller things, but that will help you reach your long-term goals (Top Budgeting Myths, n.d.).

Budgeting Is Boring

Not everyone will enjoy the menial task of figuring out all the bills and earnings and sorting them, but if you particularly dislike making a budget, you could think of it as a chore that you can't forgo, like laundry or washing the dishes. No matter how much you try to delay the chores, you will have to do them in the end. As time passes, you might even start to enjoy the planning part, especially if you buy a planner and stationery to make it fun. At the end of the day, it isn't the most exciting or interesting task, but doing it will allow you to have financial freedom (Ramsey Solutions, 2022).

I Don't Have Enough Money to Budget, So Why Bother?

Budgeting isn't just for people who have a lot of money; in fact, it works better for people who have limited earnings because it helps you maximize your earnings (Top Budgeting Myths, n.d.).

How To Establish a Budget

There are a few different ways you can create your budget, but typically, there are 2 main budgeting strategies that people use: zero-based budget and envelope budget. And while these are very popular strategies, they might not work for everyone. It is a good idea to try it out, but you will need to modify them accordingly.

Zero-Based

Zero-budgeting basically means that you will divide the entirety of your salary or income until nothing is left. This doesn't mean that you will spend all of your money; instead, everything you earn will have a dedicated place and purpose, so no penny is left behind. The first thing you will do is list all your expenses and figure out how much you spend or want to spend on a single category. The next thing you need to do is subtract your expenses from your income, so everything equals zero. If you end up with a negative number, it means that you are spending more money than you earn, and, in this case, you need to cut back on your expenses (Ramsey Solutions, 2022).

The problem with zero budget, or really any budget, is that you need to constantly monitor your expenses and keep track of your transactions. But quite a few apps can help you with this problem. Then, you need to create a new budget every month, changing it slightly according to your preferences (Ramsey Solutions, 2022).

People usually compare the zero budget to the 50/30/20 budget, but they are quite different. The 50/30/20 budget basically means that 50 percent of the income goes towards your needs, 30 percent goes towards the things you want, and 20 percent goes towards your savings. While this is quite easy to navigate, the budget leaves a lot to be desired. First of all, these percentages don't change no matter what personal struggles you are dealing with, so it isn't flexible. Additionally, the budget considers debt a need, and you can only make minimum payments. So, if you are looking for a more flexible budgeting system, try giving the zero budget a go (Ramsey Solutions, 2022)

Envelope Budget

Envelope budgeting is a cash-based system that was created to help people who have a hard time sticking to a specific financial limit. When you are paying for things using your cards, it is easy to distance yourself from the money you are spending. A cash-based budget helps you get in touch with how much you are actually spending. You take a few envelopes and dedicate each one to a separate category. Assign cash to each category, depending on how much you plan to spend. Once the cash runs out of a particular envelope, you cannot use any more money until the next month comes around. This allows you to take a deeper look into your spending and avoid going over budget by helping you track your spending. However, there are a few disadvantages to this type of budget. It can be more time-consuming than other methods, it's not as secure as using a credit or a debit card, and the chances of theft or scams are higher (Lake, How Does the Envelope Budgeting System Work? 2022).

Tip # 26:

Use the envelope budgeting method if you are someone who isn't very good at tracking expenses, or cannot resist your debit or credit cards.

A General Guide on How to Budget

Starting any new project can be overwhelming because there is so much conflicting information online. To make your life easier, here are nine steps to help you establish the most efficient budget.

Step 1- Determine Your Income,

First of all, you should evaluate your monthly income, so you know how much money you have to work with. This can be taxing to some because they have multiple income sources, which aren't always consistent. If you have your own business, you need to set aside a portion of the earnings each month for your own salary, so your spending money is separate from the businesses. If you don't get paid monthly but annually, you must divide the money by 12 (Caldwell, 2021).

Step 2- List Categories of Mandatory Expenses

The second thing you need to do is make a list of all the typical expenses you make every month. This list can include all the bills, such as rent, electricity, water, heat, and internet, and also all the other expenses you make to sustain yourself, such as food, health insurance, medications (if you take any), and transportation (Caldwell, 2021).

Step 3- List Categories of Discretionary Expenses

Next, list all the things you usually spend money on but aren't really necessary in your life. They are things that you want but don't often need. For example, things like a gym membership, home décor, personal grooming, eating out, subscription services, and clothing, among many other things. You can also include any other contributions you make, such as contributions toward your emergency fund and or retirement account. You will not have any problems if you scale back on these expenses for a little while, but you don't need to worry; these things aren't being removed from the budget. Once we figure out a fixed financial contribution that you will be making towards each item, these things can move to the mandatory expenses list (Caldwell, 2021).

Tip # 27:

Don't be a victim of advertising and marketing. Advertisers know how to get your attention and make you want what they're selling. To avoid impulse buying, don't use shopping as a way to relax or unwind from the stresses of work or home life. Don't shop on impulse — if something catches your eye, wait until later when you have time to think about it before buying it. For items you really do need or want, look for sales and special offers.

Step 4- Estimate Expenses

Now that everything is down on paper, start by assigning values to each item on the list. Just make an educated guess about the amount of money you spend on each category (Caldwell, 2021).

Step 5- Compare Estimate and Actual Expenses

Get hold of your spending history for the last three months and figure out how much you actually spend each month. You can take help from your bank statements and receipts to get this right. Compare the values with the estimated numbers, and if you find a major discrepancy, you need to focus on minimizing your spending (Caldwell, 2021).

Step 6- Assign Spending Limits Within Your Income

Once you make sense of how much you are spending each month, it's time to set limits. Start with mandatory expenses and then add the values up and subtract them from the total earnings. The amount that is left can be spent on discretionary expenses and reaching saving goals. But don't spend all the money; make sure that a set value is assigned to each category, and these categories include saving and retirement funds (Caldwell, 2021).

Step 7- Look for Places to Cut Expenses

If you are going over your monthly earnings, you need to find areas from which you can cut back on expenses. Start by lowering the amount you spend on discretionary activities and cut back on that. You can then find ways to cut down on money in your mandatory expenses and do it by spending less on food, taking communal transportation services instead or driving, etc. if for some reason you aren't able to make ends meet, then it may be time to get a second or a different job (Caldwell, 2021).

Step 8- Track Your Spending

Now that the budget is established, stick to it, and stop spending money in each category once you reach the spending limit you have set for yourself. If you want to spend more on one category, you can transfer the money from any other category; however, you cannot add more to the budget itself (Caldwell, 2021).

Step 9- Plan for The Next Month

Taking the initial step is the hardest, and once you start with budgeting, it will become easier for you as time goes by. Just examine how you spend your money each month and make adjustments according to your spending (Caldwell, 2021).

Tip # 28:

Consider using a budgeting mobile app for increased convenience. Budgeting apps help you keep track of their spending and plan ahead for their future goals, making the process of managing finances much easier. Most budgeting apps come with features such as automatic notifications when bills are due, so you'll never miss a payment and can stay on top of your financial situation without needing to constantly manually check in.

Setting Up an Emergency Fund

An emergency fund is exactly what it sounds like; you set aside some of your monthly income for unplanned expenses like home or car repairs or medical bills. An emergency fund is essential if you wish to have a strong financial plan. It helps you take care of any unwanted expenses and helps you avoid being in debt. Without a fund, you won't have any choice and will have to fall back on taking high-interest loans or using credit cards (Investopedia, 2022).

A common question that arises when people are starting an emergency fund is how much money is enough. An emergency fund typically covers 3 to 6 months of expenses, which means covering the basics, not replacing your total income. But figuring out how much to save isn't as easy because individual situations complicate the process, so before you get on with saving the money, here are a few questions you need to consider (Investopedia, 2022).

- How many people do you support or are in your household?

- How many people work in the household?

- What is the minimum amount of money you need to cover all your expenses?

- How stable is your monthly income?

The number of people you support, and the stability of your income really affect how much you can put into your emergency fund. Always remember to keep the amount realistic (Lake, How To Create An Emergency Fund, 2021).

Tip # 29:

"Keep your emergency fund separate from your checking account because you don't want to accidentally dip into those savings."

When Should I Use My Emergency Fund?

Emergencies can pop up anytime, and no matter how much you prepare for them, they will always be stressful. The least you can do for yourself is set up an emergency fund to lessen the mental and physical burden caused by the emergency (Bennet, 2023). Back when I was working one of my first jobs, I accidentally tripped and fell down a flight of stairs, breaking my ankle in the process. I was able to get immediate medical attention, but because I had a fracture, I had to give up several weeks of work until I made a full recovery. So, I went into planning my budget for the next couple of months and realized I would have enough money to cover my expenses because I already had an emergency fund going. It wasn't enough to cover all my expenses, but I just had enough to get by so I could focus on recovering my body as quickly as possible. No one could have predicted the accident, but having an emergency stash of money to fall back on really saved my sanity.

Aside from the personal situation I illustrated, there are a few other times it's applicable to use your emergency fund. An emergency fund can be used for basic expenses after a job loss or a demotion, pay for any major car damage repairs after an accident, and help with emergency house repairs. Aside from that, you can also use your emergency fund to pay for any unexpected travel, especially if you have to visit a sick loved one or if someone has passed away (Irby, 2022).

Tip # 30:

Ask yourself these 3 Questions before dipping into your emergency fund:

» Is this an important or a normal expense?

» Do I need to get my hands on this money immediately?

» Can I use other resources to collect cash for this particular expense?

How To Build an Emergency Fund

Building your emergency fund isn't as complicated as it seems. There are only 5 major steps you need to follow to succeed at saving for a rainy day.

1. Set Several Smaller Goals

Instead of trying to save for six months from the start, try setting a one-month goal first. Setting smaller goals and reaching them keep you motivated so that you can continue saving money (5 steps to building an emergency fund, n.d.)

2. Start Small and Be Regular

Be realistic about the amount of money you can contribute each month. Start by saving a small percentage each month and then increase it as your income grows (5 steps to building an emergency fund, n.d.).

3. Automate Your Savings

The easiest way to save money is by automating it, so it is directly deposited in your account as soon as you get your income. This is why it is a good idea to set up a completely separate account for your emergency fund (5 steps to building an emergency fund, n.d.).

4. Don't Increase Monthly Spending or Open New Credit Cards

People often forget to update their saving amount as they grow in their professions. So, if you have a lot of extra money at the end of the month, perhaps you should consider upping the amount of money you put into your savings and emergency accounts (5 steps to building an emergency fund, n.d.).

5. Don't Over-Save

Don't be overambitious and divert too much of your income toward your savings. While saving larger chunks of money can be easier, it isn't financially feasible for most people. Plus, your emergency fund is probably in a low-interest account, so you can avoid paying additional charges on it, so over-contributing might just devalue your money instead (5 steps to building an emergency fund, n.d.).

Now that we have reached the end of the chapter let's look at an example of a budget planner so that you can better understand how to structure it.

Budget Planner

Accommodation	Personal	Food	Debt	Transportation	Saving
Mortgage	Internet	Takeout	Student debt	Public transport	Retirement fund
Electricity	Hobby	Grocery	Car loans	Petrol	Emergency fund
Water	Alcohol	Dine out	Credit card expenses	other	
Telephone	Other	Other	Health insurance		
Gas			Other		
Total:	Total:	Total:	Total:	Total:	Total:

Keep in mind that budgets will look different for everyone depending on what their goals are and what they wish to prioritize.

Summary

- Set up a savings account because it helps you limit debt, gives you financial freedom, and helps you save money for retirement.

- It is a good idea to prioritize your savings before spending the money on bills.

- Cook meals at home and cancel unused memberships to save money.

- Open high-yielding savings accounts instead of regular savings accounts because they give you higher interest rates.

- Set up a side hustle to earn an extra source of income.

- Start budgeting to monitor and control where and how you spend your money.

- Budgeting will take extra time and effort, but it is totally worth it.

- Aside from a typical savings account, you should also set up an emergency fund for unpredictable expenses or incidents.

- The amount of money in your emergency fund will vary depending on how many people you support.

- Before using your emergency fund, ask yourself if this is the right situation to use it and whether this expense can be postponed.

- Start by saving small amounts of money and setting smaller goals because when you reach a goal, you feel motivated to continue saving money.

4–BANG FOR YOUR BUCK

Thomas Jefferson once stated that you should never spend your money before you have it, and he was absolutely right. Many people make the mistake of buying things that they don't necessarily need simply because they like them, after all, they will get paid next month. But this behavior is not sustainable, and it also messes with your budgeting so while you will be satisfied at that moment, it will cause you a lot of long-term problems. Keeping this problem in mind, chapter 4 will be focusing on the concept of opportunity cost and how it affects spending. We will also be touching on how to spend money wisely.

Opportunity Cost

Opportunity cost means giving up goods or services to buy what you want. Consider that you set aside some money to go on a trip with your friends. You go on the trip and spend 500 dollars. Now that you have spent the money, you can't spend more money on anything else. This doesn't necessarily mean that you are spending your money wrong, it simply means that you have no other way of utilizing the money once it has already been spent on something else (Opportunity Cost, n.d.).

> **Tip # 31:**
>
> One way to make the most out of opportunity cost is to be mindful of your spending choices and try to maximize each dollar spent. For example, if you are deciding between two investments, you should only decide after doing thorough research on both opportunities and weighing their potential returns. It can be beneficial to look at which option has lower risks as well as higher rewards so that you can avoid any financial losses due to a lack of knowledge or wrong decisions.

Spending Money Wisely

Almost every adult has to learn how to spend money wisely on their own because unfortunately, this isn't a skill people teach you in school. Many families aren't comfortable discussing money-related issues and problems at home either, which is why a lot of adults have a hard time with budgeting and tend to overspend. Learning how to spend money wisely is essential for achieving financial independence. When you are living with your parents, you have something to fall back on, so your income isn't disposable. However, transitioning into an adult requires a lot of reflection and focus regarding how you spend your money. Not only do you have to pay the mortgage, but you might also have to pay your student loans, car installments, credit card bills, and any other living expenses you have. When you learn how to spend your money properly, you can figure out how to structure your budget and take control of your financial situation (Laney, 2022). Here are some tips for spending money wisely.

> **Tip # 32:**
>
> To make sure your money stretches as far as possible, make sure to prioritize the essentials like housing and food first, then allocate funds for other items such as entertainment, travel, or clothing.

Track Your Spending Habits

It is easy to go over your budget if you aren't monitoring your spending habits. People don't keep track of their spending because it's tedious and takes a lot of time. But technology has made it much easier for us to keep a record of all the money we spend. There are quite a few ways you can do this, but the most common is an expense tracker. Expense trackers come in many different forms, and choosing one depends on how you spend money. If you prefer to keep things simple, you could write down your spending on a piece of paper or keep a small diary of expenses. However, if you find it tedious to write everything down, you can download apps that let you sync your bank account with your tracker, so everything is automatically imported, categorized, and tracked (Miller, 2022).

> **Tip # 33:**
>
> It can be helpful to track spending by writing down all of the purchases you make in a budget journal, app, or spreadsheet. This will give you an accurate view of what you're spending your hard earned money on each month.

Identify Areas to Reduce or Eliminate Spending

If you are falling short on cash each month, you might think that you just aren't earning enough, but that is not always the case. Sometimes we make unnecessary expenses, and we don't realize how much of our hard-earned money these expenses are consuming. Before you start thinking about getting another job or setting up a side hustle, here are some ways you can cut down on your spending.

Update Subscriptions

People sign up for multiple subscriptions over the course of a year and these subscriptions include anything from streaming services to publications and gym programs. But if you haven't used these subscriptions in the last three months, it's time to get rid of them. If cutting them completely out of your life seems unfeasible, check if you can sign up for a cheaper alternative. You can always resubscribe when you are in a better financial situation (Milliken, 2022) (Morris, 2023).

Save On Utility Costs

You obviously can live without water and electricity, but you can find ways to lower the cost of your bills. Here are some ways you can do it:

- Replace your bulbs with LED bulbs. They cost a little more initially, but they last longer and use a lot less electricity.

- Invest in a thermostat that can either be programmed or controlled via an app. This will allow you to lower your heating and cooling system when you aren't home thus, saving money on utility bills.

- Unplug electrical devices when they are not in use.

- Turn extra lights off when you leave a room or your home.

(Morris, 2023)

Consolidate Debts

If you went to school and drove your own car, then you might still be paying off some student debt and or car loans. These monthly payments can eat away at a large portion of your earnings because you are probably paying a minimum of 16 percent interest on those debts. The best way to lower the amount you pay in interest is by consolidating your debt. This refers to combining multiple debts into one monthly payment so that you can reduce the interest and pay the debt off as soon as possible (Milliken, 2022).

Shop For Cheaper Insurance

There are plenty of companies that offer low-cost car or medical insurance with just as many benefits and we often miss these because we don't research before settling on an insurance plan. Now is the time to search for different companies that offer low-cost insurance or bundle discounts (Morris, 2023).

Eat At Home

Preparing meals at home can be very tedious which is why people choose the convenience of takeaways and deliveries. But these food deliveries can pile up over time and make you spend a lot more than you initially planned on spending on food. You can start by preparing a meal plan and then buying and prepping groceries on the weekend. This will make it much easier for you to put food together. You could also cook meals for the entire week, freeze them, and consume them throughout the week (Milliken, 2022).

Shop With a List

We tend to get distracted and buy things we don't really need when we are grocery shopping. To minimize the money you spend on unnecessary things, you should always shop with a list. This is a very simple habit, but it can help you drastically cut down on food expenses and also help with meal planning. Keep adding to a list throughout the week and when it is time to go grocery shopping, divide the items into categories so that they are easier to grab once you are in a specific aisle (Milliken, 2022).

Cheaper Housing Options

One of the biggest expenses you will make is on housing and if you are spending a lot of money on it, maybe it is time to downsize. However, if that isn't applicable to your situation there are a few other things you can consider, namely getting a roommate or moving to a cheaper area in your region (Milliken, 2022).

Understand The Difference Between Wants and Needs

Understanding the difference between wants and needs can be one of the most challenging steps because it varies from person to person. It is easy to confuse your wants with your needs if you are accustomed to them. Wants aren't inherently a bad thing, in fact, they can often help you accomplish personal goals but often, they are unnecessary to your well-being. Some examples of needs are utility bills, rent, healthcare and therapy, medication, commuting, and food, and some examples of wants are dining out, buying new clothes, traveling, entertainment, monthly subscriptions, and streaming accounts (Pant, 2022).

If you want to be financially independent, it is important to understand the difference between needs and wants. Being able to differentiate between the two things can help us make better financial decisions and ensure that we are using our money responsibly. It also helps us prioritize our spending and set aside funds to save more effectively. In addition to all of that, it also helps you avoid falling into expensive debts by minimizing your spending so that you only buy what is necessary (Pant, 2022).

Apply Smart Shopping Practices to Save Money

If you feel like you run out of money as soon as it is deposited in your account, you might have a spending leak. These impulsive and unnecessary purchases may seem small, but they can add up and once you stop spending money on these purchases, you will be surprised to find out how much extra money you have saved (Plug Your Spending Leaks, n.d.).

Tip # 34:

Plug Spending Leaks: Spending leaks, also known as lifestyle creep, occur when small expenses which are not noticed or tracked begin to add up over time. These are the extra coffees bought here and there and the little items that keep appearing in your shopping cart without you even noticing.

The most effective way to plug up your spending leaks is to track everything you spend. Note down the money you spend and keep receipts to ensure accuracy. Once you identify the financial leaks, you can work on plugging them. Examine each purchase and expenditure and ask yourself if this is something you actually need and how much money it costs you every month. These questions can help clear up any doubts you might have about the expense and help you decide if it is worth continuing or not. If you don't want to completely cut the expense out of your life, it might be beneficial to consider any alternatives that provide you with value but have a lower cost. Using coupons and making use of sales is one of the best ways to enjoy things while still staying within your budget (Plug Your Spending Leaks, n.d.).

Tip # 35:

Research before making large purchases and always look at more than one source of information. A good place to start is by reading online reviews of the product. People who have already purchased the item can provide honest feedback on whether or not they would recommend it, as well as insight into some potential pitfalls or things that may be improved upon.

Tip # 36:

Be creative and look for alternative solutions to expensive items or services. Take a look at your spending habits and make sure you're taking full advantage of budget-friendly solutions for everything from transportation to housing

Review and try to find cheaper alternatives for everything, especially if you are on a limited budget. For example, if you frequently take taxis and Uber, consider choosing public transport instead. Not only will you save quite a bit of money, but this is also a lot more sustainable for the environment. Using public transport also saves you the headache of trying to hail a cab. Similarly, if you spend a lot of money on buying lunch every day, maybe you can switch to packing your own lunch, which is much cheaper but tastes just as great. When it comes to buying clothes, try looking at the alternatives such as thrift clothes or second-hand goods. Used items not only cost a lot less money but you also find one-of-a-kind pieces. You can continue to keep your wardrobe up to date, without having to break the bank.

> ### Tip # 37:
>
> **Be proactive about searching for deals, discounts, and rewards programs.**

If you know where to look, you will be able to find unlimited websites that are dedicated to finding discounts. You could even check out social media platforms like Twitter and Facebook to find deals. Joining the email list of retailers is another great way to find discounts and deals. Some stores even offer coupons that can be used in-store or online and they further reduce the cost of items. Additionally, many credit card companies offer reward points for each purchase you make, and these points can be used to buy merchandise or gift cards or can be spent on travel expenses.

> ### Tip # 38:
>
> **Ask friends and family for advice before making major purchasing decisions.**

Asking friends and family before you make big financial decisions can be very effective since it helps you evaluate whether the products are worth investing in. Friends and family usually provide us with honest feedback about their experiences with the product and give us a realistic idea of how the item performs. When asking questions, make sure to target important questions such as how did the product help you? Or would you recommend this product? I remember a couple of years ago when I was buying a laptop, I asked my friends and family about the best laptops in my price range since they might know laptops that are good quality. Initially, I wanted a laptop that was low priced because I wanted to use it for simple tasks, but my uncle suggested that I buy another model that cost a lot more than I wanted to spend. He assured me that the laptop was very good quality and following his advice, I bought the laptop. I still use the laptop today and am still surprised at how well it works. I didn't even need to repair it or replace any parts. It is safe to say that from that time on, I consulted my family every time I made a big purchase.

Tip # 39:

Wait at least 24 hours before making a decision to buy something to avoid impulse purchases.

When you are buying something, you aren't just spending your hard-earned money but also your time and energy. If you don't weigh the pros and cons every time you buy something, you will end up buying things that aren't necessary. The solution? The 24-hour principle. The 24-hour principle basically means that if you want to avoid impulse buying and the remorse and guilt that follows, then you should give yourself at least 24 hours before deciding if you want to make the purchase, especially if it is a bigger one. When we make immediate decisions, we often base them on emotions rather than logic and emotions can overpower our logic but if you give it 24 hours, the logic will kick in and take over. After the 24 hours pass and you still want the product then perhaps you should buy it and if you are no longer interested, it might have been a passing impulse that you definitely would have regretted later down the line. The best thing about this principle is that it lets you mull over the purchase and decide if it is worth it. (How waiting 24 hours can avoid buyer's remorse, n.d.).

Spending Freeze Challenge

- If you want to save money fast, then perhaps you could try the freezing challenge. But how exactly do you partake in the freezing challenge? Here is what you need to do:

- The first thing you need to do is set the duration of the challenge so start small and do the challenge for about a week. During these 7 days, you will not be spending any money at all. Think about possible ways to overcome this instead of trying to come up with excuses.

- Start on Sunday and continue till Saturday. Don't put pressure on yourself, if you can't complete it this week, maybe you can try again next week.

- Don't spend any money. This includes eating out, groceries, washing your car, getting a babysitter, or any other thing you usually spend money on.

- Utility bills are generally not included in the spending freeze challenge.

- Spending on gas is up to you. Some people consider gas as a need rather than a want. If it isn't a bill or unexpected expense, you need to wait until the freezing challenge is over in order to spend money on it.

(Page, n.d.)

Summary

- It might be a good idea to adopt the opportunity cost mindset so that you can stay within your budget.

- Spending wisely is an essential part of achieving financial independence.

- Always keep track of all your spending.

- Identify areas where you can reduce the amount of money you spend.

- Look into finding a cheaper alternative to subscriptions, eating out, and housing, among other things.

- Understand there is a difference between needs and wants.

- Ask your friends and family for their honest advice.

5—BREAK THE BANK

"There are three kinds of people: the haves, the have-nots, and the have-not-paid-for-what-they-haves." - Earl Wilson

The last few chapters have talked about setting up good habits so this chapter will target why people fall into debt and explore the different types of debts. It will also provide you with strategies to overcome it and discuss how you can establish good credit and repair bad credit.

Debt

Debt is basically the money one party borrowing from another party in order to accomplish a goal. Usually, bigger corporations, like banks, let people borrow money so that they can make large purchases that they couldn't afford in normal circumstances. The money is borrowed under certain rules and has to be paid back with a certain amount of interest within a limited time (Chen, 2022). However, there are some other reasons people fall into debt so let's discuss some of them.

Low Income or Underemployment

People who don't earn a lot of money, and fall under the low-income group, might not have enough money to pay all their bills since all of their money goes into sustaining themselves (Furniss, 2016).

Divorce And Relationship Breakdown

When couples get divorced, their income drastically reduces. Plus, people need tons of money to go through divorce proceedings (Furniss, 2016).

Poor Money Management

People who don't budget, save, or prepare for emergencies are the ones that are most likely to fall into debt. This is why people need to keep an eye on their bank accounts and spending and cut back if they are financially overstretched (Furniss, 2016).

High Costs of Living

Aside from inflation in general, some people also have the misfortune of living in expensive areas in the country. This means that people generally have higher house prices, longer commutes, and rental demands (Furniss, 2016).

Overuse Of Credit Cards

Credit points or interest-free credit deals sound exciting; however, people can quickly fall into debt if they don't routinely pay off their card bills (Furniss, 2016).

Declining Health and Medical Expenses

Healthcare is very expensive in most countries and people who are sick are also unable to work. This is exactly why medical expenses are the most common cause of debt. The sad thing is that some illnesses are not the result of negligence but rather they are unfortunate accidents so it isn't something people can avoid (Furniss, 2016).

Unexpected Expenses

Accidents happen so having savings or a good insurance policy is essential. However, many people are trying to survive day to day, so they don't really have the luxury of an insurance policy, nor do they have extra money to set aside for an emergency fund (Furniss, 2016).

Job Loss

Having a regular salary provides a lot of financial security so when people do end up losing their job, they are unable to pay bills and fall into debt (Furniss, 2016).

Living Beyond Your Means

Education And Student Debt

Almost everyone who goes to college has a student debt they need to pay so a large portion of the money is deducted from every paycheck you earn. The only good thing is that this type of debt doesn't affect people's credit scores (Furniss, 2016).

Having Children

While having children is an experience every parent wants to have, it is no secret that children are extremely expensive. This is often why some people fall into debt when they first start providing for their children (Furniss, 2016).

Failed Business and Business Expenses

Starting a new business can be a very big step for many people but many businesses fail to gain mainstream attention which causes them to fail. As an owner of a business that has gone under, you might have a lot of debts (Furniss, 2016).

Good Vs Bad Debt

Unlike popular belief, some debt can be considered good debt if it has the potential to increase your overall net worth. Mortgages, student loans, or debts you incur to start your own business are all examples of good debt. On the other hand, if you are incurring debt to buy a depreciating asset, then you are accumulating bad debt. Cars, clothes, and other consumables are examples of bad debt (Smith, 2023).

Tip # 40:

Set your sights on the lowest interest rate possible. In addition to reducing the amount of money you need to pay back each month, it can also have a positive effect when it comes time to file your taxes.

Ways To Avoid Debt

Debt is something that sneaks up on you but that doesn't mean that you can't limit the possibility of falling into debt. Here are some ways to avoid debt.

- Budgeting is great because it not only helps you track where you are spending your money but also helps you fully utilize every penny you earn. So, if you ever have to decide to cut down your expenses, you know exactly which areas to target.

- If you have to fall back on your credit card to have cash, then you are abusing your finances and you need to cut back on your expenses.

- One of the most dangerous things you can do to yourself is fall under the misconception that you can afford something simply because you have a credit card, even if you don't necessarily earn enough to cover the expense. So, if you can't pay for it in cash, then you can't afford it.

- Paying via a card can quickly get out of hand so use cash whenever it is possible.

(10 Strategies to Avoid Getting into Debt, n.d.)

Tip # 41:

Avoid lifestyle inflation. Avoid the trap of upgrading your lifestyle whenever you get an increase in income.

Strategies For Paying Off Debt Quickly

Trying to get rid of your debt can be very overwhelming since you don't really need to know where to start. While there are no right or wrong ways to get rid of debt, there are a few methods that can work for you. The most popular methods are the avalanche and the snowball methods (Comparing the snowball and the avalanche methods of paying down debt, n.d.)

Snowball Method

The snowball is a debt reduction strategy that encourages you to pay off your debt by starting from the smallest to the largest. It is one of the most popular and effective ways of getting rid of debt since it lets you set up a timeline. This method works for people because it seems the least daunting. You see continuous results that keep you motivated so that you can keep paying off debt as quickly as possible. Snowball only works if you have a small amount of debt so if it doesn't work, try the avalanche method. (Ramsey Solutions, 2022).

Tip # 42:

If your total debt load is large, it may be better to focus on attacking the highest interest-rate loans first no matter what order they are in.

Tip # 43:

Be honest about your budget - having a realistic view of what you can truly afford each month is key when trying to decide if this approach will work for you.

> ## Tip # 44:
>
> Know yourself and keep yourself motivated - even though the snowball method takes time and dedication, it can help give an individual motivation by showing them progress as they start paying off their loans one at a time.

Avalanche Method

The avalanche method is the opposite of the snowball method. You can start with the debt that has the highest interest rate and pay it off first while paying the minimum on the rest. This is a very effective way to minimize the overall interest while working on getting rid of all your debts. This method works best for people who can afford to make more than the minimum payment each month and tackle multiple debts simultaneously. Creating a budget and monitoring the progress helps you stay organized so that you can continue to make payments each month (Smith, 2023) (Zinn, 2022).

> ## Tip # 45:
>
> Use the avalanche method when you have multiple debt obligations and prioritize reducing your total amount of debt over the speed of repayment.

Credit

Credit is the credit history of an individual or a company. The credit helps you make deals with the bank and determines whether you will be able to get a car loan, student loan, or mortgage. Credit scores are essential even if you don't necessarily want to buy something and many people look at your credit score to determine if the people, they are dealing with can be trusted. So, bad credit naturally suggests that you are a risk and people will avoid dealing with you (Dieker, 2022). Let's discuss a few major benefits of maintaining good credit.

Lower Interest Rates

One of the major benefits of maintaining good credit is that banks offer you a lower interest rate on your loans, credit cards, and even mortgage. This is because lenders use your credit scores to determine the interest rate (VanSomeren, 2021)

Improved Likelihood Of Qualifying For A Loan Or Credit

It is quite discouraging when you are denied a mortgage or loan since most people depend on it to make their dreams come true. Good credit can improve your approval odds so that you never have to experience that disappointment (VanSomeren, 2021).

Approval For Certain Jobs

Some jobs that involve handling money naturally require you to go through a personal credit check, so a good credit score is necessary to land such jobs (VanSomeren, 2021).

Larger Credit Card and Loan Limits

A better credit score helps you get approved for larger loans as well as higher credit card limits (VanSomeren, 2021).

Better Credit Card Rewards

In addition to all the other benefits, a good credit history also helps you access a lot of amazing credit card rewards (VanSomeren, 2021).

Easier Approval for Rental Properties

A lot of property owners do a background check of their credit history before considering rental applications so in order to get a good apartment, you need a good credit score (VanSomeren, 2021).

Lower Insurance Rates

Insurance companies also check your credit history before accepting you as a customer and decide how much interest they will charge you (VanSomeren, 2021).

Negotiating Power on Loan Terms

Credit scores can not only help you get lower interest rates, but they can also help you during the mortgage negotiation process (VanSomeren, 2021).

Types Of Credit

There are a few different types of credit. Let's explore them and their differences.

Installment

Credit is basically when you borrow a fixed amount of money from a lender and pay the lender back within a limited period of time. These types of credit include student, car, or other personal loans (Bringle, 2021).

Open

Credit doesn't really have a hard limit and payments are usually based on how much you use the cards. Utility bills are often part of open credit scores, and the payments can affect your score (Bringle, 2021).

Revolving

Credit can be borrowed again and again up to a limit set by the lender. The best example of revolving credit is the credit card (Bringle, 2021).

Your credit score is based on a variety of different things such as the payment history, the amount you owe, the duration of your credit history, and your credit mix, which is exactly why you need to have a good credit history in all three types of credit (Bringle, 2021).

Tip # 46:

Having some variety in your account types can indeed be beneficial when it comes to maintaining a good credit history, as long as you are mindful of how much debt and usage each type of account carries. When it comes to having a good credit mix, it is important to remember that less is often more.

Establishing Good Credit

Now that we have reiterated the importance of good credit, Let's explore some ways you can build good credit.

Review Your Credit Reports

Before you can work on your credit history, review your credit report so that you can identify areas of improvement (Lake, 2022).

Only Borrow What You Can Afford

A credit card isn't a superpower that suddenly allows you to buy everything you have ever dreamed of. It is simply an extension of your paycheck that allows you to make bigger purchases in advance, but those purchases should still be something you can afford. This is why you should only borrow the amount you can pay back (Irby, 2022).

Use Only a Small Amount of Credit You Have Available

Maxing out your credit card is just as irresponsible as using your credit card to buy things you cannot afford. People who max out their credit cards often end up having difficulty paying off their debt so be responsible with your shopping (Irby, 2022).

Tip # 47:

As a guideline, use no more than 30% of your credit limit (using less is even better for your score).

Start With Only One Credit Card

Credit cards are addicting but you have to pay a maintenance fee for almost all the cards. This is why you should avoid making the mistake of opening too many cards too soon and stick to exploring one card (Irby, 2022).

Pay Your Credit Card Balance in Full

When you pay off the bill each month, it shows the bank that you are fully capable of paying the bills. This helps you maintain a good credit score (Irby, 2022).

Make All Your Payments on Time

Any bill can end up ruining your credit history. To prevent that, you need to pay all your bills on time (Irby, 2022).

> ## Tip # 48:
>
> To avoid late payments, set up autopay, check your statements regularly, and set reminders on your phone to help you make all your payments before the due date.

If You Carry a Balance, Do It The Right Way

Having a balance isn't a bad thing as long as you continue to pay the minimum amount each month to get rid of the balance quickly (Irby, 2022).

Let Your Accounts Age

A longer credit history is better for your credit score so use one account if possible and keep it open as long as possible (Irby, 2022).

Repairing Bad Credit

Bad credit can affect a lot of different areas of your life. For instance, having a poor credit score can be detrimental if you are hoping to buy a car, a home, or take out a loan. Not only do people with bad credit histories miss out on life-changing opportunities, but it can also affect your hiring or renting prospects. To avoid this, you need to maintain a good credit history by staying up to date with payments. But if you have already damaged your credit history, here are some ways you can rebuild it (Kurt, 2021).

Check Your Credit Report for Accuracy

Look at your credit history to identify places that can be rebuilt or improved (Improve or rebuild credit, n.d.).

Tip # 49:

To ensure your financial health is always in check, consider ordering one of your credit reports every 4 months from a different reporting company. Monitoring this regularly can help identify and address any concerns that may arise promptly.

Dispute Any Errors in The Credit Report

After checking your report, dispute any information that is either inaccurate or doesn't belong to you (Improve or rebuild credit, n.d.).

Pay Every Account on Time

At least try to make the minimum payment on all the debts you owe and reduce the overall amount (Improve or rebuild credit, n.d.).

Avoid Taking on A New Debt

If you already have bad credit, try to minimize the amount of credit you use (Improve or rebuild credit, n.d.).

Maintain Low Balances Apply for A Secured Credit Card

Typically, a secured credit card is for people who want to build credit from scratch. But it is great for people who have had their credit cards closed and need to start building their history from the bottom (O'Shea, 2022).

Tip # 50:

Keeping your unused cards open can give you a credit boost. Maintaining an extended length of credit history and utilizing your available credits responsibly both play important roles in building good scores (Improve or rebuild credit, n.d.).

Summary

- Not all debt is bad debt. Student debt can actually be considered very good and improve your credit history.

- In order to avoid debt, you should evaluate your spending habits and stick to a budget.

- You could either use the snowball or avalanche method to pay off your debt quickly.

- Good credit is essential if you want to take out a loan or mortgage.

- All three types of credit contribute and create your credit history.

- To repair your credit history, you should pay your accounts on time and maintain a low balance, among other things.

6–FLOAT A LOAN

"I will forever believe that buying a home is a great investment. Why? Because you can't live in a stock certificate. You can't live in a mutual fund." –Oprah Winfrey

Loans are a significant part of human existence since they allow people to further their studies and buy homes. So, in this chapter, we will be providing a detailed outline of different kinds of loans and how to manage and pay them off.

Loans

We have already touched on loans in the previous chapters but just to remind you, loans are basically a sum of money that a party lends out to another party in exchange for a set amount of interest (Kagan, 2021). Loans have a lot of benefits but just as many disadvantages. The pros of loans are that there are a lot of different types so there has to be one that suits your needs. Additionally, you can improve your bad credit with loans and consolidate different loans to lower the interest rates. On the other hand, you might not get any loans if you have bad credit and even if you do get the loan, you will have to pay tons of interest on it (Gregory, 2021).

There are many different types of loans such as personal, auto, student, mortgage, home equity, debt consolidation, mortgage, small business, title, boat, and land loans. In this chapter, we will be discussing student, mortgage, and auto loans.

Student Loans

Student loans basically pay for all your tuition fees, living expenses, or any other fees you may incur while going to an accredited school. Anyone who studies after high school is saddled with student debt. In fact, as of 2022, about 45 million Americans struggle with student debt (Kurt, 2022). The most common type of student loan is a direct loan, and it can be either subsidized or unsubsidized. When a loan is subsidized, the federal government is responsible for paying any interest on those loans unsubsidized loans, on the other hand, require the borrower to pay interest (Lake, 2022).

Managing Student Loans

Tip # 51:

If you are struggling with managing student loans, try to make use of deferment and forbearance.

Deferment

Both deferment and forbearance allow you to postpone loan payments temporarily. However, you can put them in effect in different situations. During the duration of the deferment, you won't have to pay any principal loans but if you have unsubsidized direct loans, you must pay the interest by yourself, or it will be added to the overall balance. Some qualifications for deferment are unemployment, financial hardship, enrollment in school, active military duty, serving in the peace corps, and rehabilitation programs due to disability. There is no set length of deferment, the duration is determined by the different types (Porter, 2022).

Forbearance

If you aren't eligible for deferment, you might be eligible for forbearance. Typically, you can apply for forbearance for up to 3 years, for 12 months at a time. This can help relieve the financial burden for a short period of time, but you must think ahead of time. Applying for reduced payment will pause your payments and make sure that your debts don't get out of control. However, one major drawback of forbearance is that your debt continues to add interest so at the end of the forbearance period, the interest is capitalized (Deferment and Forbearance, n.d.).

Payment Options

Now that we have talked about student loans and some key aspects, let's talk about the different payment options.

- Standard repayment- Borrowers pay their loans in the shortest period of time to limit the interest and the loans are paid off over 10 years.

- Graduated repayment- This kind of payment starts off lower but increases in amount until the loans are fully paid.

- Extended repayment-These loans are paid over a period of 25 years. You will benefit from this if you have a larger loan and want to pay smaller monthly installments.

- Pay As You Earn (PAYE) plan- This payment plan takes monthly payments at 10 percent of the discretionary income and never exceeds the payment for the standard repayment plan.

- Revised Pay As You Earn (REPAYE) plan- Monthly payments are set so that you pay 10 percent of your discretionary income.

- Income-Based Repayment (IBR) plan- payments are set at either 10 or 15 percent of your income but you never pay more than you would have on the standard repayment plan. You might be eligible for loan forgiveness after 20 to 25 years of payments.

- Income-Contingent Repayment (ICR) plan- The amount is set at 20 percent of your discretionary income or the amount you would pay over 12 years.

- Income-Sensitive Repayment (ISR) plan- Payments are based on your annual income and loans are paid over 15 years.

(Lake, Student Loan Repayment Options: What's the Best Way to Pay?, 2022)

> ### Tip # 52:
>
> **One tip for student loan repayment is to pay more than the minimum monthly payment.**

Consolidating Student Loans

To lower the interest rate, you can combine multiple loans together and consolidate them into one payment so that you only make one payment per month. There are many benefits of consolidating such as access to repayment plans, federal benefits, and lower monthly payments. You will enjoy the benefits of lower interest rates while having a 30-year flexible repayment period (Bareham, 2022).

Auto Loans

Auto loans are exactly what they sound like, instead of taking out a loan to pay for whatever you want to buy, car loans are taken out specifically to purchase a car. Interest on car loans is much lower since the lender isn't taking much of a risk and can seize the car if the borrower fails to make any payments (Probasco, 2022). However, in order to qualify for a car loan, you need to have good credit, a verifiable income, and a low debt-to-income ratio.

Good Credit

The lender will review your credit and determine whether you are trustworthy or not. A good credit score is usually set at 670 or higher. You might be able to get better deals and a lower interest rate if you have a good credit score (Correa, 2022).

Verifiable Income

To get an auto loan, you will have to show that you will be able to repay the loan. This means supplying the lender with your financial information and your overall income (Correa, 2022).

Low Debt-To-Income Ratio

Your debt-to-income ratio is the amount you owe in monthly debt payments. In order to be considered for a car loan, your DTI needs to be higher than 50 percent (Correa, 2022).

Where To Get a Car Loan?

There are two possible ways to get an auto loan: direct lenders and dealership in-house financing. Direct auto financing is a car loan that can be available through banks, credit unions, and other online lenders. Dealership in-house financing, on the other hand, is accessible through the car dealership itself. In direct lender situations, you will be able to shop around for the best deals, get pre-approved, and pick the perfect deal. Indirect financing, however, works a bit differently. You will go to a car dealership, select a car and then talk to the in-house auto loan service and work out the details. One major drawback to this is that the dealers will increase the interest rate (Bank Rate, 2022).

Tip # 53:

Ask any potential lender about their repayment terms and what kind of additional perks or protections they offer—some may even provide gap insurance or extended warranties for extra protection down the road.

Car Financing Vs Car Leasing

When you lease a car, you are paying to drive it for a certain period of time, with the average being 24 to 36 months. You are restricted to make modifications and can drive for a limited number of miles. After the period is over, the car goes back to the dealership. Car financing, however, basically means you are buying the car and you are the owner of the car in all aspects. You pay monthly installments to your loan provider until your car is fully paid off. Car leasing means that you have to make smaller payments, lower expenses on maintenance, and better tax deductions. Buying a car means that you own the car once the payments are made, there are no limits to the miles you drive, you can modify the car however you want, and you build equity on the car. Both car leasing and financing have their benefits and choosing between them depends entirely on what you are looking to get out of the vehicle (Benoit, n.d.).

Tip # 54:

Make sure you understand the mileage allowance of your lease agreement and keep track of your driving habits when selecting the right contractor for you.

How To Get an Auto Loan?

To get the best interests on your auto loan, you need to follow these steps.

Check Your Credit Report

Your credit score and income will determine how much you can borrow and if you can borrow in the first place. This is why you need to apply after checking your credit report.

Apply For Auto Loans from Multiple Lenders

Check out multiple lenders so that you can compare quotes and get the best rate.

Get Preapproved for An Auto Loan

Once you have narrowed down lenders, it is time to pick the correct lender and get pre-approved. Getting pre-approved means that you will get an estimate of the rate and the loan you will be qualifying for, based on your credit history.

Use Your Loan Offer to Set Your Budget

Your pre-approved offer will tell you the maximum amount you can borrow but that shouldn't dictate what car you will be buying. You need to put aside at least 10 percent for any additional expenses.

Find Your Car

Once you have settled everything else, it is time to pick out the car. Make sure to check lender requirements, time restrictions, excluded brands, and dealership requirements to minimize disappointment.

Review The Dealer's Loan Offer

Once you have checked the car and confirmed that it matches your needs, you can indulge the car dealership and review their loan offer. If you go in with a preapproved loan amount, the dealer might try to beat the rate and get you a better deal.

Choose And Finalize Your Loan

Now, carefully evaluate the bank and the dealership's offers and select which one you might be leaning towards. Make sure to ask about hidden fees, longer loan terms, and gap insurance.

Make Payments on Time

After the loan payment is in effect, you are free to enjoy your car. However, make sure to make the car payments on time since these can affect your credit history.

Mortgage

Buying a home or even renting out a new home is a very big financial decision, and you need to make sure that you are ready for it before you take the plunge. Be it moving to another town or staying within the same one, being aware of the costs can help give you peace of mind before you make such a big move. Aside from the financial aspect, you also need to consider all the important information since so much is at stake, both emotionally and financially. So, before you decide to either buy or rent a home, explore the pros and cons of both things.

Buying Vs Renting: Pros and Cons

Pros Of Renting a House

One of the major pros of renting a house is its affordability. This is exactly why renting is a much more realistic option for people since most people have limited funds or are just starting their careers. Plus, if you decide to move or upgrade to a bigger home, you will not have to worry about selling your property. Another major pro of renting a house is its flexibility. When you are renting, you don't have any long-term commitment to the house and can typically get away with signing shorter leases ranging from 6 months to a year. This is great for quick changes of locations if you need to move due to employment or any family situations. You can also shop around for the perfect house since you don't have to worry about an expensive longer agreement. Lastly, rentals are easier to maintain since landlords take care of the upkeep of the property. These include any structural damages, plumbing issues, or replacement costs, saving the renters a lot of time and money they would have spent if they were the owners (Comai-Legrand, 2019) (Majaski, 2022).

Cons Of Renting a House

One major downside of renting a house is that tenants have very little control over the changes they might want to make to the property so they can't really personalize it. Additionally, you will also not build any equity on the house and all the payments go towards paying for someone else's assets rather than contributing towards your own. In addition to that, renters also have very limited security since the shorter agreements give the landlords the power to decide if the lease will be renewed or not after the agreed period is over. This means that you could be forced to leave your home at any given moment. Lastly, owners can enter your space at any given moment, unless specified otherwise, so the tenants have limited privacy (Comai-Legrand, 2019) (Majaski, 2022).

> ### Tip #55:
>
> **When it comes to securing a rental property, preparation is key. Take the time prior to searching for your new home to compile all necessary documents such as income statements and references so that you can move quickly when making an offer on your dream house.**

Pros Of Buying a House

Owning a house has a lot of benefits. First of all, you build equity in the house over time. You okay the mortgage and make improvements, which increases the value of your home over time. Secondly, owning a home offers a lot of stability and consistency, which renting can't. You can change the house however you want and don't have to get approval from your landlord. This allows not only freedom but also peace of mind. In addition to that, owning a house brings in a sense of pride and people strive their entire lives to make it happen. Plus, homeowners also offer certain tax benefits like deductions on property damage, interest rates, and a lot of other things, which can result in significant savings over a period of time. Lastly, buying real estate is one of the safest forms of investing money since property values only increase over time so, there is a lot less risk as compared to other types of investments like bonds and stocks. Both bonds and stocks are stable because they lose money due to market fluctuations and changes in interest rates (Comai-Legrand, 2019) (Majaski, 2022).

Cons Of Buying a House

A major downside of owning a house is the cost of maintenance, taxes, insurance premiums, etc., since all of these need to be paid even if you are experiencing financial difficulty. In order to avoid getting overwhelmed by these multiple payments, you need to budget ahead of time. Selling your house later down the line may also pose a problem, especially if the conditions are unfavorable due to an economic downturn. Real estate prices also fluctuate over time and as a house owner, this can be both positive and negative. Additionally, homeowners need to be thoroughly educated in all financial aspects of managing a house since all the expenses needed to maintain the house will come out-of-pocket. Lastly, just as being a homeowner brings stability, it also requires you to be responsible, which might not suit everyone, especially people who enjoy freely changing residences and abhor "being tied down" by long-term obligations (Comai-Legrand, 2019) (Majaski, 2022).

Tip # 56:

Homeownership is a rewarding experience but like with any new endeavor it can be intimidating. To make sure your journey is as successful and fulfilling as possible, remember this one key tip: maintenance!

Basics Of Mortgage

A mortgage is basically a very specific type of loan that is taken out in order to purchase land, a home, or any other kind of real estate. Similar to other kinds of loans, this type also requires you to pay off the borrowed money as well as principal interests over a period of time. If you are unable to pay, your property serves as the collateral. Most mortgages are fully amortizing, which means that the payments will stay the same, but portions of principal and interest will be calculated and added to each payment. Traditional mortgage terms are 15 to 30 years (Kagan J. , 2022). There are many different kinds of mortgages, so let's discuss them.

Conventional Loan

Conventional loans aren't backed by the government and are either conforming or non-conforming. Conforming loans conform to the standard set by the FHFA. Non-conforming loans, on the other hand, do not meet the standards set by the FHFA but cater to borrowers who want to purchase more expensive homes or people with unusual credit profiles (Marquit, 2022).

Jumbo Loan

Jumbo loans fall outside the FHFA borrowing limits and are common in high-cost areas such as New York, Hawaii, LA, and San Francisco. It allows you to purchase more expensive homes and the interest rates tend to be competitive with conventional loan rates (Marquit, 2022).

Government-Insured Loan

The government doesn't issue loans, but it does back some lending agencies to make housing more accessible to citizens. The government backs three agencies: the FHA, USDA, and VA loans. The FHA loans have competitive interest rates and make housing possible without having to put down a large downpayment. The USDA loans help moderate-to-low-income citizens and help them buy homes in rural areas. Finally, VA loans are providing low-interest rates, and flexible mortgages for people who are serving in the US military (Marquit, 2022).

Fixed-Rate Mortgage

A fixed-rate mortgage, or a traditional mortgage, functions by keeping the interest rate stable throughout the loan term. Since the interest doesn't change, neither does the monthly payment towards the mortgage (Kagan J. , 2022).

Adjustable-Rate Mortgage

The interest rate of the adjustable-rate mortgage will stay fixed for an initial term, but it can change periodically based on current interest rates. The initial rates are much lower than the market rate, which might seem affordable at first, but the long-term rates rise substantially, so keep that in mind (Kagan J. , 2022).

Steps On How to Get A Mortgage

If you are wondering how to get a mortgage, here are the steps you need to follow.

Step 1 - Strengthen Your Credit

To get the best interest rates, you need to show that you are a responsible person to the lenders so create a favorable credit history (Martin, 2022).

Step 2 - Know What You Can Afford

Everyone dreams of owning a home but sometimes, dreams don't match reality. This is why you need to figure out what you can realistically afford, keeping in mind that you will be paying the mortgage off for a long time (Martin, 2022).

> ### Tip # 57:
>
> **Explore your options with an online mortgage calculator! Online mortgage calculators like the one you can find on www. mortgagecalculator.org make it easy to figure out how much you can afford for a house and get started on the path toward homeownership.**

Step 3 - Build Your Savings

The first thing you need to do is save for the down payment on the house. You also need to build up your reserves so that you have at least 6 months' worth of savings stored away in a bank. This will cushion your mortgage for a while, in case you lose your job (Martin, 2022).

Tip # 58:

A 20% down payment on your mortgage is associated with numerous financial benefits, such as a more favorable loan rate and the immediate creation of substantial equity.

Step 4 - Choose the Right Mortgage

Choose the right kind of mortgage for your situation. Don't immediately decide, it is okay to investigate and shop around for the best deals (Martin, 2022).

Step 5 - Find A Mortgage Lender

Once you decide on the type of mortgage you want, find the correct mortgage lender. Make sure to speak to your friends and family and ask for referrals (Martin, 2022).

Step 6 - Get Preapproved for A Loan

It is a good idea to get pre-approved for the mortgage once you find a suitable one. In this preapproval, the lender will check your finances to determine if you will be able to pay back the loan. Additionally, they will decide on the amount they will lend you (Martin, 2022).

Step 7 - Begin House Hunting

After you get pre-approved, start your search for the perfect property. Find a house that is feasible in your price range (Martin, 2022)

Tip # 59:

When you are entering the world of homeownership, make sure you have accounted for more than just your mortgage payments.

Step 8 - Submit Your Loan Application

Once you find a house you are interested in, complete the mortgage application. It can be done online but it is more efficient to enlist the help of a loan office (Martin, 2022).

Step 9 - Wait Out the Underwriting Process

Even if you are preapproved, you might not get the loan immediately. The final decision will come from the underwriting department since they evaluate the risk associated with each prospective borrower (Martin, 2022).

Step 10 - Close on Your New Home

Once you get approved for the mortgage, you are almost at the finish line. All you need to do is close on the home. Keep in mind that there are a lot of fees that come with closing the house so you might need to set some money aside beforehand (Martin, 2022).

Summary Box:
Top Tips for Mortgage Shopping

Tip # 60:

Knowledge is power. Make sure to do your research and become well-versed in the different types of loans and mortgages that are available. Knowing your options, and which type of loan is best for you will give you more leverage when negotiating terms with potential lenders.

Tip # 61:

Make sure to shop around and compare lenders. Look into banks, credit unions, FHA loans, VA loans, USDA loans, mortgage brokers, and any other sources that may provide financing for your needs. Speak with multiple lenders about their rates and fees so that you know exactly what each one is charging for similar services.

Tip # 62:

Assess your credit score before applying for a mortgage or loan. If you have a good credit score, then you're likely eligible for lower interest rates on your loan; if not then it may be harder (or more expensive) to secure a mortgage.

Summary

- Don't miss payments on your student loans. Instead, apply for deferment or forbearance.

- There are many repayments plans for student loans so choose the one that benefits you.

- Consider consolidating student loans to keep the interest rates lower.

- Get pre-approved for a mortgage and a car loan.

- Figure out whether you want to finance a car or lease it.

- Figure out whether you want to rent or buy a house by looking at the pros and cons.

- Choose a property you will be able to afford in the long-term.

7–SITTING ON A GOLDMINE

In the words of Robert Allen, "How many millionaires do you know who have become wealthy by investing in savings accounts? I rest my case." It is quite obvious that just saving money will not allow you to build your wealth. In order to do that, you need to invest money. The previous chapters focused on managing debt, saving, and spending wisely, so this chapter will focus on building your own wealth and talk about the different kinds of investments.

Basics Of Investment

Investing is the process of buying resources that grow in monetary value over time and provide you with income in the form of payments or capital benefits. In general, investing is used to improve the holder's quality of life, however, in the larger sense, finances basically provide the person with a lot of security and guarantee gains. In the most basic sense, investing works by buying an asset at a much lower price and selling the same thing when it increases in price (Curry, 2022). Before you can start investing, there are a few things you need to keep in mind, let's discuss them.

Safety

While there is no such thing as a safe investment, you can minimize the damages by taking a few extra steps. First of all, you should invest in government-issued securities if the economic situation of your country is stable. The only way you will lose your money is if your government collapses. If not, you can get AAA-rated corporate bonds that are issued by large corporations. Aside from that, you can also invest in treasury bills, T-bills, commercial paper, banker's acceptance slips, and certificates of deposit (Hayes, 2022).

Income

Some people are looking to buy assets that guarantee them a stable income, so they are ready to be a little riskier. This is mostly seen in people who are retiring or retired and want to generate a stable income that keeps up with inflation. The best investment for these people is government or corporate bonds as well as AAA-rated choices (Hayes, 2022).

Capital Growth

Capital growth can only be attained by selling your asset. Capital growth doesn't just refer to property but it also includes diamonds or other things that increase in monetary value (Hayes, 2022).

What Is Your Investment Style?

Making sense of your investment style is the best way to find out which investments out of the thousands you might be interested in (Fontinelle, 2022).

Active Vs. Passive Management

Before finding out your investment style, you need to consider if you think financial experts will be able to get you better investments. Investors who want to have money managers carefully evaluate their holdings and are interested in active management. These managements have staffs full of financial researchers and portfolio managers who seek to gain the best returns for their investors. These firms charge a lot of money because you are not only paying for investment but also the expertise of the staff. Passive management, on the other hand, gets better returns for the investors so you don't necessarily need researchers or fund experts, which is why the prices of passive management are low (Fontinelle, 2022).

Growth Vs. Value Investing

The next thing the investors need to consider is whether they want to invest in fast-growing funds or underpriced industries. The people who prefer growth investing look for firms that have high earning growth, high profit, low dividend yields, and high return on equity. People who prefer value investing focus on buying a strong firm at a stable price. So generally, they look for a low price-to-sales ratio, higher dividend yields, and a low price-to-earnings ratio (Fontinelle, 2022).

Small Cap Vs. Large Cap Companies

The last thing you need to consider is if you want to invest in smaller or larger companies. Measring the size of the company is called "market capitalization," which is basically the shares of stock a company has after it has been multiplied by its share price. People who prefer small companies think that they have better returns and more opportunities to grow. People who prefer larger corporations, on the other hand, find comfort in depending on large stable companies since they are more trustworthy and have been around for a long time (Fontinelle, 2022).

Types Of Investment

There are many different kinds of investments so let's discuss them in detail.

Stocks

Stocks are basically equities and give shareholders a chance to own a part of the company. If you have more shares in the company, you control how it operates and which direction it takes. But where exactly does the stock come from? public companies present stocks to the general public so that they can find investors to find their business. Investors who think that the company might be successful buy their funds and invest in their business (Royal, 2022).

Stocks can become a very valuable part of your portfolio and they can help you build your savings and protect your money from taxes and inflation, all while maximizing the profit from your investments. There are typically two main types of equity investment, and both have different benefits. the first stock type is the common shares. They are often available for Canadian investors, and they offer capital growth, liquidity, voting privileges, dividend income, and advantages in tax treatment. the second type is the preferred shares. These provide a very realizable stream of income as well as a much higher income in general. In addition to that, prefer shares also have a lot more variety, each with different features (Key Benefits of Investing In Stocks, n.d.).

The problem with investing in stocks is that they fluctuate rapidly so some companies may not do well and go bankrupt and if that happens, you will lose all your money. Another major disadvantage is that stocks are very expensive, especially if you invest in a larger company so many people can't really afford it (Royal, 2022).

Tip # 63:

Before investing in stocks, it's important to understand and assess your own risk tolerance.

Bonds

Bonds are a form of debt security. When you buy a bond, you are lending your money to an issuer and these issuers can be the municipality, corporation, or government. In return, the issuer pays you a specific interest on those bonds, during their entire lifetime and pays you the entire bond back when it matures. People generally diverge towards bonds because they provide a consistent and predictable income. Plus, the issuer guarantees to pay all the money back after the bond matures so there is a sense of security (Bonds, n.d.).

There are a few risks to investing in bonds. First of all, there is an interest rate risk which basically affects the value of the bond. If the bond is allowed to mature, you get the principal amount back but if you take it out before time, it may be worth less than the face value. In addition to that, there is always the risk of inflation so while your money is stored away in bonds, they might be devaluing. Lastly, there is also a possibility that the issuer will retire the bond before it matures and this generally happens when the interest rate declines (Bonds, n.d.).

Tip # 64:

To maximize your returns, you should always research the creditworthiness of the issuers and evaluate the maturity date of each bond.

Mutual Funds

Mutual funds are when a company combines money taken from different investors and invests that money in stocks, short-term debt plans, or bonds. These combined funds are the portfolio of the company, and each share represents part ownership of the fund. Mutual funds are very popular for a number of reasons. First of all, mutual funds have professional managers who do the investment research for you. Secondly, they invest in multiple different companies and ventures which helps lower the risk of the investment failing. Additionally, mutual funds are a lot more affordable than stocks and have very low investment value. Lastly, mutual funds can be easily redeemed which earns people the right to get their shares at any time without any repercussions (Mutual Funds, n.d.).

Like all investments, mutual funds also have their downsides. You may lose all your money in investments because the securities held by funds can decrease in value. dividends and interest rates also change as the market situation changes. Past performance doesn't guarantee future returns, but it can tell you how stable or volatile a fund is, so keep that in mind (Mutual Funds, n.d.).

Tip # 65:

Be mindful of your investment time horizon- determine the amount of time you plan on holding onto your investments.

Real Estate

We have already talked about real estate in detail in the last chapter but let's go over why it is a good idea to invest in real estate. The main thing that drives people towards real estate is that real estate appreciates over time, so long as you target the right market. Real estate also has very unique tax benefits that allow investors to grow their wealth over time. Additionally, real estate provides you with a monthly income that is passive but allows you to keep building your business while spending time with family and reinvesting in real estate (Lyons, 2023).

Just like real estate has advantages, it also has disadvantages. Real estate requires a lot of upfront investment before you can start reaping the benefits, so it isn't for everyone. Real estate also takes a lot of time, and it is a long-term investment that most people aren't ready to make. In addition to all of this, real estate also has a lot of risks since it is easy to buy or sell the property at the wrong time, which can cause you to lose money (Lyons, 2023).

Tip # 66:

Start small. Investing in real estate doesn't always require a large upfront investment; you can purchase smaller properties or shares of larger ones, as well as enter into joint ventures with other investors who may have more capital available.

Cryptocurrency

A cryptocurrency is basically a form of digital currency that isn't backed by any official authority or real assets. It is a form of trade between consenting parties without a broker. Out of all the cryptocurrency sites, bitcoin is the most popular one. It can take many forms, ranging from investing in crypto funds and companies or buying it directly. The biggest benefit of bitcoin is that it is very affordable, and you can get very high profits. Investing in cryptocurrency is very risky because even the most established ones can be volatile, and if in the future it becomes illegal, it will be worthless. But crypto is developing rapidly so if you want to invest in it, you need to keep the changes and developments in mind (Garnett, 2022).

Tip # 67:

Crypto markets are open 24/7 so set limits on yourself as far as when you invest and how much you are willing to invest per transaction in order to avoid impulsive decisions that may have drastic consequences.

Retirement Accounts

401 (K) is one of the only retirement savings plans offered by the US government and it has many tax advantages for the saver. The person who agrees to this plan agrees to have a percentage of their paycheck deposited directly into an investment account and the employer matches that part or the entire contribution to the employee's funds. Employees also get a chance to choose a number of investment options. There are two main types of 401 (K) investments: traditional 401(K) and Roth (K). In traditional plans, the employee contributions are deducted from the gross income, which is the income before tax deductions. So your taxable income is reduced by the number of contributions each year and you don't have to pay any taxes on the money until you withdraw it. In Roth 401(K) your contribution is deducted from your income after the tax. This means that you won't get any tax deductions in the year of contributions. But your money will be tax-free when you withdraw it at the end (Fernando, 2023).

Tip # 68:

Review your current contribution rate periodically and adjust as needed according to the changes in your savings goals or income level.

Inflation And Your Portfolio

Inflation is when the prices of goods and services rise due to the decrease in the purchasing power of the currency. This means that the same amount of money no longer holds the same value. While it may seem simple, inflation can have far-reaching consequences. Inflation can have both a positive and a negative effect on investment portfolios. It encourages investors to seek out investments that have higher yields so they can keep up with the rising price. Plus, if your portfolio includes investments that benefit from inflation then those investments will obviously appreciate over time. On the other hand, inflation can cause you to lose on certain investment types due to lower returns. It also erodes the value of income over time because when the prices rise, the consumers have to pay more for the same goods that they used to purchase at a lower price. It reduces consumer buying power and forces them to find ways to make a living within their budget. Inflation also reduces the risk of any potential future earnings since wages tend to not keep up with the increased cost of living (How Does Inflation Affect Your Finances, n.d.).

Tip # 69:

Having assets that are not subject to inflationary pressures can help keep your overall returns from being eroded by inflation.

---

4 Strategies to Mitigate Risk During Volatile Economic Times

Since the pandemic, people have started to experience bigger periods of limited market volatility which means that no one is safe from hard times. If you find yourself in an unfavorable situation, here are 4 ways you can mitigate the risk (Reciprocity , 2021).

Diversify Your Assets

One simple way of lowering risk is to avoid making all your investments in the same company or sector. Diversify your assets so that even if you lose in one area, you get stability and gains in the other (Reciprocity , 2021).

> ## Tip # 70:
>
> **It is essential to diversify your stock portfolio not only across types of investments but also across different industries, companies, and countries.**

Hedge Your Investments

Hedging is an investment strategy that helps you minimize losses if your stock value falls. You hedge your investment by purchasing an option that gives you a right to sell your stocks if it dips below a specific price (Reciprocity , 2021).

Stay Informed

Keep yourself up to date with the market changes and how fluctuations affect investments. You won't be able to predict the future, but it will give you a vague idea of when to hold, buy, and sell your assets (Reciprocity , 2021).

Wait It Out

If your stock value dips, don't freak out immediately. Minor changes are common and have a temporary effect on your assets so you will be able to weather them over time. Before selling, observe how the market usually functions and figure out if you want to hold or sell (Reciprocity , 2021).

Investing in your financial future is important, but it's also crucial to protect yourself and your family with the right insurance. When you're ready to expand your financial knowledge beyond investments and loans, learning about the basics of insurance can help you make sure you're covered in case life throws an unexpected curveball.

Summary

- Consider the safety of an investment, your income, and overall capital growth before investing.

- Stocks can become a very important part of your investment portfolio.

- If you invest in bonds, wait until it matures so that you can take full advantage of them and minimize any losses.

- Mutual funds are a great way to invest money since your money is invested in multiple different areas.

- Investing in real estate is one of the best decisions but it does require a large amount of money, so it isn't for everyone.

- Inflation causes a lot of problems for consumers so while you are investing, make sure you aren't losing any money to inflation.

8–AT A PREMIUM

This chapter will focus on the importance of insurance because, "you don't buy life insurance because you are going to die, but because those you love are going to live." We will also touch on different tips that can help you shop around for the right insurance company and plan.

Insurance

Insurance is a contract between the policyholder and the company in which the company provides financial protection or reimbursement in case of a loss and in exchange the policyholder provides the company with a sum of money each month. Before you can choose a company or a policy, you need to understand how insurance works and three main components of insurance are crucial in understanding how it functions (Kagan J. , Insurance: Definition, How It Works, and Main Types of Policies, 2022). Let's discuss them.

Premium

The premium of a policy basically means the monthly cost of that policy and it is determined by examining your business risk. For instance, if you own expensive cars and have a history of reckless driving and accidents you will pay more money for the insurance policy as compared to someone who has a perfect record. But different companies charge differently for the same policy, so you need to ask around before picking a single company (Kagan J. , Insurance: Definition, How It Works, and Main Types of Policies, 2022).

Policy Limit

The policy limit is the maximum amount of money a company will pay to the insured to cover their loss. The maximums can be set annually, per policy term, over the life of a policy, and per loss or injury. Higher policy limits naturally mean higher premiums (Kagan J. , Insurance: Definition, How It Works, and Main Types of Policies, 2022).

Deductible

The deductible is the amount a policyholder needs to pay before the company starts covering the damages. These serve as deterrents to large volumes of smaller claims. The deductibles are applicable per claim or policy, depending on the kind of policy. Policies that have high deductibles are less expensive since you are paying for a lot of it out-of-pocket (Kagan J. , Insurance: Definition, How It Works, and Main Types of Policies, 2022).

What Kind of Insurance Do You Need?

The future is unpredictable, so we must be prepared for any and all unfortunate incidents. Insuring against life-changing losses should always be a priority when choosing an insurance policy. There are four main kinds of insurance policies that you might want to invest in: life insurance, health insurance, auto insurance, and disability insurance (McMaken, 2022).

Life Insurance

Life insurance is important if your family depends on your income to survive or if you have a debt that will pass on to your family if you die. The older you get, the more expensive your life insurance becomes and that is why you need to buy life insurance when you are younger, especially if you can get it at a lower rate. The right time to buy insurance will obviously vary from person to person, depending on both the family and the financial situation (Tracy, 2023). There are two main kinds of life insurance policies: whole life and term life.

- A whole life policy can be used as an income tool and an insurance instrument. It has death benefits and cash value. As the value of the policy increases, you can either access the money by taking out a loan or taking out the cash value of the policy and ending the policy.

- Term life policy covers you for a fixed period of time like 10, 20, or 30 years. This is the most affordable type of policy.

(McMaken, 2022)

Generally, people should get life insurance when they are younger, but it isn't possible for some because of pending student loans, mortgages, and other kinds of loans. If you aren't planning on having a partner and kids, then you might not need an insurance policy. However, if you think that it might be a part of your future, then you need to get the policy before you have an apparent need for it (Tracy, 2023).

> **Tip # 71:**
>
> **Don't be afraid to shop around and compare multiple companies and their offerings.**

Health Insurance

Most people don't think they need health insurance because they never get sick, but no one plans for sickness or an accident, it is always unplanned, so it is better to prepare for the worse than wait for it to happen and then struggle to make ends meet. A broken leg can cost you more than 7,500 dollars to treat and that doesn't include the medication, the hospitalization, and the rest of the expenses. Having this kind of medical debt can cripple you for a long time. The proof of the unpredictability of life is obvious since no one could have predicted the pandemic and it caused a big financial upheaval that was difficult to handle. With the rising cost of healthcare and inflation, people have started struggling even more and the only thing you can do for yourself, and your family is to plan for turbulent times. Medical insurance is not only necessary to protect yourself and your family from unplanned diseases and injuries, but it also helps you protect your savings by making sure that they are used for their intended purposes and not to cover medical costs (6 Reasons Why You Need To Get A Health Insurance, n.d.) (Why bother with health insurance?, n.d.).

Tip # 72:

If you're young and healthy, look into high-deductible health plans (HDHP).

Auto Insurance

I remember one time I was driving for hours because I wanted to reach my destination before sundown. I had a thanksgiving dinner scheduled with my family and had promised them I would be there, so I wanted to keep my word. My car started to run low on gas and I remember pulling into a small town nearby so that I could find a gas station and fill my car up. Unfortunately, just as I pulled my car into the main street of the town, a delivery truck came out of nowhere and slammed into my car. I very fortunately avoided getting seriously hurt but my car was badly damaged. The only thing that gave me peace of mind is that I had auto insurance and knew that it would cover all the damages. This situation came out of nowhere and if I didn't have car insurance, I would have had to pay that money out of pocket and most likely fallen into debt. However, if you aren't convinced to buy car insurance, here are a few reasons you should consider it.

- First of all, not having car insurance is illegal in most US states so you kind of have to invest in it. In fact, if you don't have it, you might have to pay some hefty fines.

- Insurance doesn't just protect you; it also helps you pay for any accidents that you may have caused.

- Having car insurance also protects your assets because if you don't have enough money to cover the expenses, the other person's lawyer might seize all your assets in order to pay the damages.

- If you are found to be at fault for the accident, then you not only cover your own expenses but also have to pay for your passenger's bills and medical bills can be very expensive.

(Butsch, 2022)

Home Insurance

Our homes are the biggest investments we make in our lives. It's not just the property that is valuable, it is also the belongings and the memories that are attached to that house. But sometimes, even the best security systems fail to protect our homes from natural disasters, accidents, fires, and theft because we can never eliminate the possibility of something happening. However, we can minimize the financial impact these accidents may have by getting home insurance. There is no legal requirement for it and you don't need it if you are renting the property, but if you own the house, it might be a good idea to invest in it. You could get the standard policy which covers hail, wind, smoke, explosion, and fire damage, as well as damage caused by criminal activity. You could also choose building insurance which covers the walls, the fixtures, and fittings, or go with content insurance which covers items inside the home such as laptops, jewelry, pictures, furniture, and so on (Why Is It Important To Have Home Insurance?, n.d.)

> ## Tip # 73:
>
> There may be discounts available that could further reduce your insurance costs.

Disability Insurance

Disability insurance covers people who are unable to work. The decision to buy this insurance depends on your financial situation so if you are unable to work and don't have any other source of income to cover your living costs, disability insurance can really help make your life easier. To qualify for this insurance, you must have been employed in a job that required you to pay into social security and you must have a medical condition that meets the definition set by social security. If you are partially or temporarily disabled, then you aren't qualified for this insurance. There are two main types of private disability insurance:

- In the short-term policy, you need to wait for 14 days, and the benefits pay for almost 2 years.

- In the long-term policy, you need to wait for a few weeks or months but the benefits payout for a few years up to the receiver's lifetime.

(Do I Need Disability Insurance?, n.d.)

> ## Tip # 74:
>
> Make sure you understand any exclusions in the policy and what types of disabilities are covered (for example, mental health issues versus physical disabilities) your disability insurance.

7 Tips for Choosing the Right Insurance Company For You

Choosing the right insurance company and plan can be quite overwhelming, so to make it easier, here are a few tips that you should follow while looking for your insurance policy.

1. Compare the reputation of companies

The good thing about living in a digital age is access to reviews left by previous customers. Make use of these reviews and find out how long they have been in business, which states they cater to, their mission and values, their financial strength, and their company leadership (Stueber, 2016).

2. Understand the insurance company's financial strength

You never want to be in a difficult situation only to find out that your insurance company cannot afford to pay you. Many companies work with external companies that rate their agencies so look for those reviews (Stueber, 2016).

3. Financial coverage

Pick an insurance company that can provide the amount of coverage you need for your business or personal needs (Stueber, 2016).

4. Prices

Price should be an important consideration, but it shouldn't be the only one. Sometimes, you get what you paid for. If you pay a lower price, then you will have less coverage so you will have to pay more money out of pocket. Talk to your insurance agent before selecting the lowest price right out of the bag (Stueber, 2016).

5. Easy of doing business

Your insurance provider should make you feel comfortable enough that you don't hesitate to ask them any important questions. So, choose a company that doesn't make you feel awkward or stupid (Stueber, 2016).

6. Discounts

Many insurance companies may offer discounts so ask whether you can apply for those discounts or not. Also, make sure to ask any appropriate questions that go with those discounts, such as is this discount for a limited amount of time, and will you have to pay full price after a specific time or not? (Stueber, 2016).

7. Ask for referrals

Marketing is very convincing, and it can quickly sway us in one direction. However, before settling on a company, ask your friends and family for their opinions and referrals (Stueber, 2016).

Now that you've learned all about personal finance, it's important to pass those lessons on to your children and the next generation. Teaching your children about money management is an invaluable lesson that can help them throughout their lives and give them a strong financial foundation.

<u>Summary</u>

- Make use of the internet and ask for referrals before settling for an insurance plan and company.

- Life insurance should be bought as young as possible.

- If you are partially or temporarily disabled, you don't qualify for disability insurance.

- Home insurance can help protect your memories and the items inside your house.

- You can never predict accidents so make sure to sign up for auto insurance because not only is it illegal not to have car insurance in all states, but it will also prevent you from paying a lot of money out of pocket.

146

9–ON THE HOUSE

"He who opens a school door, closes a prison." – Victor Hugo

The reason we have to learn about finance on our own is that we aren't taught finance at home or school. So, to combat that and protect your children from experiencing the same troubles, we are going to focus this chapter on the importance of teaching your children the importance of saving money, setting financial goals, and being mindful when making decisions.

Tip # 75:

Discuss Wants vs. Needs - It's never too early to teach children the importance of financial responsibility - beginning with a lesson in understanding wants versus needs. Parents can help kids distinguish, for example, between essential basics like housing and healthcare and 'extras' such as movie tickets or designer accessories. By introducing these fundamental concepts at an early age, we are setting them up for long-term success.

> ## Tip # 76:
>
> Let Them Earn Their Own Money - Instilling the importance of saving starts in childhood. Giving children a chance to earn and keep their own money is an effective way for them to learn budgeting skills and recognize the value of hard work.

Benefits Of Starting Them Young

Kids may seem too young for this kind of conversation, but they are very intelligent and soak up everything you teach them. By talking about money, you are giving them valuable financial information. Aside from that, there are many other advantages of teaching them young.

- For many, money is a taboo topic that demonizes money itself and can make people afraid of using it. occasionally talking about money can help normalize conversations about money and make it seem like a means to live a good life, instead of the end goal.

- Teaching them skills will help them reach financial success later in life.

- You could turn your past mistakes into life lessons, so your kids don't make the same mistakes.

- If you don't teach them, there is a chance they might never learn.

- Many adults struggle to manage their finances so teaching your children financial education can help them grow into financially confident adults.

- Money is a very mentally challenging topic for some so if you teach your children how to manage money young, they can lessen the anxiety surrounding money later in life.

(4 Reasons it's Important for Kids to Learn Financial Literacy, 2022) (Payne, 2022)

Tip # 77:

Set Savings Goals - Helping children understand the power of saving can be a great way to cultivate good habits. Introducing kids to savings goals that are achievable and relevant is key – such as breaking down larger amounts into smaller, attainable targets. With this approach, young ones will soon realize what it takes for them to purchase their desired items over time.

Tip # 78:

Provide a Place to Save - Help your children reach their financial goals with an accessible savings account! Whether they're young or a bit more experienced in the world of finance, you can equip them for success by setting up either a traditional bank account or kid-friendly debit card. Give them the tools to build healthy money habits and watch their dreams take shape.

Four Principles to Begin Teaching Financial Literacy

Four main principles can help begin the process of teaching your children about financial literacy.

Tip # 79:

Have Them Track Spending - Encourage children to take control of their finances by tracking weekly spending. Show kids how impactful small adjustments can be, helping them reach savings goals faster and more efficiently.

Tip # 80:

Act as Their Creditor - Money smarts begin young! Ensure your child learns the important lesson of saving by becoming their creditor. If they want something that costs $50 and feel impatient, "lend" them the money - with interest from their allowance payments. Delaying gratification is key: if you wait to purchase items, it'll cost less in the long run.

Tax A Little

Kids need to know that they don't keep every penny they earn. The government collects a major chunk of your earnings as tax so figure out ways to teach them how it works (Edelman, 2022).

Tip # 81:

Let them earn their own money - Encouraging your children to save involves giving them the chance to earn and manage money, which teaches them valuable skills. Providing allowances in return for completing chores also helps them understand the importance of their effort and its rewards.

Tip # 82:

Set saving goals - To a kid, being told to save, without explaining why, may seem pointless. Helping children define a savings goal can be a better way to get them motivated.

Spend A Little

One of the many joys of earning is the ability to spend it. Allow your child to buy something they want with the money they have earned (Edelman, 2022).

Tip # 83:

Let them use their saved money - Gratification is the best way to teach someone the value of something, particularly money. So, after they have reached their saving goals, let your children actually spend their money.

Save A Little

Not everything you want will appear in your hand immediately so teach your children how to save money to make a larger purchase (Edelman, 2022).

Tip # 84:

Offer incentives - If your child has set a big savings goal—for example, a $400 tablet—you could offer to match a percentage of what they have saved. As an alternative, you could offer a reward when your kid reaches a savings milestone, such as a $50 bonus for hitting the halfway mark.

Give A Little

With money, comes responsibility. Teach your children the joy of sharing their money with the less fortunate so that they can grow up to be strong and companionate individuals (Edelman, 2022).

Tip # 85:

Share with the less fortunate - Teaching children how to be responsible with money also involves teaching them that you should always share your money with the less fortunate because thats something you want them to naturally do once they start earning. You want them to grow up to be just as generous and compassionate as you are.

Tip # 86:

Welcome the mistakes! - Mistakes are not something to be afraid of. Rather they can be great for may be better to use that mistake as a teachable moment.

> ## Tip # 87:
>
> Talk about money - To instill a sense of saving in children, it's essential to maintain continuous dialogue. Whether you set aside a weekly session specifically for money discussions or integrate money talks into daily routines, the crucial aspect is to sustain the conversation over time.

7 Tips for Teaching Your Child To Save Money

Teaching children delayed gratification is one of the most important childhood lessons because it can protect them against unnecessary spending and gain complete control over their finances. Getting started can be tricky, so here are some tips that can help you.

> ## Tip # 88:
>
> Help them invest - After your children have accumulated some savings, you might explore options such as setting up a custodial brokerage account or assisting them in buying fractional shares. These avenues not only foster a sense of ownership but also impart valuable lessons on researching and overseeing their investments.

> ## Tip #89:
>
> Teach them about credit - When you take responsibility to pay back borrowed money, lenders can trust you more when you need to make a big purchase in the future.

> ## Tip #90:
>
> Help them and let them they aren't alone - You want your kids to be fully independent adults, but you might need to step in to help them from veering off course from time to time. After all, making poor financial decisions can be an expensive learning experience.

Discuss Wants Vs. Needs

Help them distinguish between wants and needs. Explain that needs are basic things humans need to live like food and shelter and want are things that we use to entertain ourselves like going to watch a movie or eating out (Lake, 2022).

Let Them Earn Their Own Money

If you want your children to save, then you need to teach them the importance of money by letting them earn it. You could make them do chores and offer them allowance as a reward (Lake, 2022).

Set Saving Goals

Set saving goals and explain why they need to save. Break their goals down into smaller steps and explain them to them so they can understand the reasons behind saving (Lake, 2022).

Tip # 91:

Set an example - Showing your kids how you achieve your goals through budgeting, saving, and investing will give them confidence that they can do the same.

Tip # 92:

Make saving visual - Who among us didn't have one of those iconic pink piggy banks during childhood? While piggy banks are a timeless concept, they lack a visual element for kids to track their savings. Opting for a clear jar instead allows children to witness their money growing, providing a tangible representation of their financial progress.

Provide A Place to Save

You need to stash your children's savings. It could be saved in the form of a piggy bank, or you could even set up savings accounts for older children (Lake, 2022).

> ## Tip # 93:
>
> Teach them contentment - With overconsumption being glorified on every single social media, it is important to teach your children how to be content with the things they have, especially if they still have a lot of life left.

Make Them Track Their Spending

A good chunk of being a saver means knowing where you are spending the money. So, help your children keep track of their spending (Lake, 2022).

> ## Tip # 94:
>
> Encourage Fiscal Accountability - Support your children in developing fiscal accountability by guiding them to track their spending. Introduce them to useful tools like a spending log or budgeting app for a comprehensive understanding of where their money is allocated. This also promotes a responsible approach to money, setting the stage for sound financial decision-making throughout their lives.

Tip # 95:

Teach them responsibility by helping them save for college - Take a portion of their paycheck to toss in a college savings account. Your teen will feel like they have skin in the game as they contribute toward their education.

Tip # 96:

Teach them about credit cards - As soon as your child turns 18, they will be hounded by credit card offers. It is up to you then to teach them the dangers and the benefits of having one before they fall victim to debt.

Act As Their Creditor

You could lend your children money if they want to buy something to teach them how loans work because learning to save also means knowing not to live beyond your needs (Lake, 2022).

Tip # 97:

Help them borrow wisely - There will always come a time when your kids need to borrow, and it's important to teach them how to do it wisely so that they don't overstretch themselves and fall into debt.

Set Good Examples

At the end of the day, children mirror their parents. They will only learn if you set good examples for them (Lake, 2022).

Tip # 98:

Set a Good Example - Setting a good example is key to leading your children down the path of saving. Showing them that putting money aside for emergencies, retirement funds or fun experiences can help instill positive financial habits from an early age. You and your family could take proactive steps towards something you all dream about - such as planning contributions in advance for special treats like a big-screen TV or vacation getaway.

Tip # 99:

Teach them budgeting - Controlling their spending means assessing where their money is going. Get them in the habit of tracking their spending by building a budget.

> ## Tip # 100:
>
> Living below means - While kids can treat themselves occasionally, make sure their spending isn't controlling them. If they cannot pay down their credit card every month, it means they are living beyond their means.

> ## Tip #101:
>
> Investing isn't gambling - Lastly, Children need to understand that investing isn't gambling. To encourage them to make smart decisions, you should allow them to invest small amounts of their money and teach them about profit and loss.

Summary

- You need to teach children about the importance of saving from a young age.

- Teach your children the importance of money.

- Children mirror their parents so set a good example for them.

- Aside from saving, teach your children the joy of spending.

These basic lessons are essential not only for the development of healthy financial habits later in life but also to understand how money works in our economy and society as a whole.

CONCLUSION

Women are already at a disadvantage because despite living in the 21st century, women are still considered inferior and completely excluded from some professional fields that are considered traditionally more masculine. Throughout this book, we have touched on various topics that can help women regain their independence and dabble in one of the most "masculine" fields, finance. Women are just as capable as men and always have been, what they lack is knowledge and this book aimed to bridge that gap by providing all the relevant information they might need in order to succeed at managing their own finances, investing, and saving for retirement or unexpected times. Each chapter is imbued with a different aspect of finance so women thoroughly explore each topic and the multitude of options they might have.

My aim with this book was to create a world where women never have to experience what I did when I was in that grocery store. That kind of shame is something that is forever imprinted in our minds. Things were quite tricky at first because I needed to curb those negative and detrimental spending habits while paying off my debts. After working hard for years and budging every single day, I finally managed to escape debt and started saving money for retirement. This newfound financial freedom gave me immense peace of mind and I no longer had to worry about piling bills. The best thing was that I didn't have to sacrifice everything to have that. Sure, some days were spent indoors, cooking my own food but those days helped me improve my overall lifestyle. I want my story to serve as a motivation for those who are also struggling with their finances. This is why each part of the book helps you contemplate your actions, what to look for, and how to use the structure of personal finance to live a better life. But understanding the why is just the start. You have to go a step further and map out steps toward success.

With this, the book has reached its end. If this book helped you and you think it can guide others who struggle with similar problems, please consider leaving a review so that the book can reach other struggling women and propel them toward financial freedom.

REFERENCES

4 Basic Things to Know About Bonds. (2022, October 24). Investopedia. https://www.investopedia.com/articles/bonds/08/bond-market-basics.asp

4 strategies for coping with market volatility. (2023, February 22). https://www.us-bank.com/financialiq/invest-your-money/investment-strategies/four-strategies-for-coping-with-market-volatility.html

4 Types of Insurance Policies and Coverage You Need. (2022, May 28). Investopedia. https://www.investopedia.com/financial-edge/0212/4-types-of-insurance-everyone-needs.aspx

5 Simple Ways to Invest in Real Estate. (2022, July 15). Investopedia. https://www.investopedia.com/investing/simple-ways-invest-real-estate/

6 Investment Styles: Which Fits You? (2022, June 5). Investopedia. https://www.investopedia.com/financial-edge/0410/6-investment-styles-which-fits-you.aspx

7 Best Ways to Build Good Credit. (2022, April 1). The Balance. https://www.thebalancemoney.com/ways-to-build-good-credit-960109

7 Ways to Establish Good Credit. (n.d.). https://www.atlanticbay.com/knowledge-center/7-ways-to-establish-good-credit/

8 Simple Ways to Trim Unnecessary Spending. (2022, January 14). The Balance. https://www.thebalancemoney.com/how-to-trim-unnecessary-spending-4129673

10 Common Money Fears and How to Overcome Them. (n.d.). Money Psychology. https://www.money254.co.ke/post/10-common-money-fears-and-how-to-overcome-them-money-psychology

10 Important Benefits of Saving Money. (n.d.). https://homebusinessmag.com/money/personal-finance/10-important-benefits-saving-money/

10 Strategies to Avoid Getting into Debt | Central Bank. (n.d.). https://www.centralbank.net/learning-center/strategies-to-avoid-debt/

10 Tips to Teach Your Children to Save Money. (2022, June 21). Investopedia. https://www.investopedia.com/personal-finance/10-tips-teach-your-child-save/

12 Easy Ways to Cut Expenses at Home. (2022, August 26). Debt.org. https://www.debt.org/advice/how-to-cut-expenses/

12 Tips to Use a Credit Card but Not End Up in Debt | Pay Off Debt. (2023, February 2). Credit Counselling Society. https://nomoredebts.org/credit/how-to-use-credit-card

54 Ways to Save Money | America Saves. (n.d.). https://americasaves.org/resource-center/insights/54-ways-to-save-money/

403 Forbidden. (n.d.). *How Your Parents Beliefs About Money Affect You.* https://www.psychologytoday.com/us/blog/mental-wealth/202108/how-your-parents-beliefs-about-money-affect-you

A. (n.d.-). *Do I Need Disability Insurance?* 360 Degrees of Financial Literacy. https://www.360financialliteracy.org/Topics/Spending-Saving/Insurance/Do-I-Need-Disability-Insurance

A Brief History of Universal Life. (n.d.). https://www.soa.org/globalassets/assets/library/monographs/50th-anniversary/product-development-section/1999/january/m-as99-3-06.pdf

A Healthy Attitude Toward Money Leads to Financial Security. (n.d.). Financial Planning Blog | More Than Your Money Inc. https://morethanyourmoney.com/blog/a-healthy-attitude-toward-money-leads-to-financial-security

A Quick Guide to Using Your Emergency Fund. (2022, January 17). The Balance. https://www.thebalancemoney.com/when-should-you-use-your-emergency-cy-fund-453900

Access Denied. (n.d.). https://www.allstate.com/resources/life-insurance/variable-universal-life-insurance

AllBusinessTemplates. (2018, May 8). *Budget Planner Printable | Templates at allbusinesstemplates.com.* Pinterest. https://www.pinterest.ph/pin/budget-planner-printable-how-to-create-a-budget-planner-printable-download-this-budget-plann--740771838683549805/

Annuity.org. (2023, January 30). *How to Set and Reach Your Financial Goals | Tips and Resources.* https://www.annuity.org/personal-finance/financial-wellness/financial-goals/

Are Your Kids Financially Literate? (2022, January 17). Investopedia. https://www.investopedia.com/ric-edelman-teach-kids-financial-literacy-4684227

Ashford, K. (2022, July 14). *The Life-Changing Magic Of Compound Interest.* Forbes Advisor. https://www.forbes.com/advisor/investing/compound-interest/

Attitude About Money. (n.d.). https://www.incharge.org/wp-content/uploads/2015/06/2-attitudes-about-money.pdf

Autobytel. (n.d.). *The Pros and Cons of Car Financing vs Leasing.* https://www.autobytel.com/auto-news/the-pros-and-cons-of-car-financing-vs-leasing-105452/

B. (2022, August 2). *IUL vs. Roth IRA: Which One is Better for Your Retirement Savings?* BravoPolicy. https://bravopolicy.com/life-insurance/iul-vs-roth-ira/

B. (2023, February 9). *Direct auto financing: What it is and how to find a lender.* Bankrate. https://www.bankrate.com/loans/auto-loans/direct-auto-financing/

Balfour, B., & Matthews, K. L., II. (2022, October 11). *How Bad Credit Affects You.* LendingTree. https://www.lendingtree.com/credit-repair/how-bad-credit-affects-you/

Bank of America | Page Not Found. (n.d.). https://www.bankofamerica.com/banking-information/error-page-en.html

Bareham, H. (2022, November 3). *Pros and cons of consolidating student loans.* Bankrate. https://www.bankrate.com/loans/student-loans/pros-cons-student-loan-consolidation/

Beal Financial Group - IUL vs 401 (K). (n.d.). https://www.bealfinancialgroup.com/iul-vs-401-k

Bennett, K. (2022, October 13). *Checking vs. savings account: What's the difference?* Bankrate. https://www.bankrate.com/banking/checking-vs-savings-accounts/

Bennett, R. (2022, September 7). *How to choose a bank: 8 steps to take.* Bankrate. https://www.bankrate.com/banking/how-to-choose-a-bank/

Bennett, R. (2023, January 11). *When should you spend your emergency fund?* Bankrate. https://www.bankrate.com/banking/savings/when-to-use-emergency-fund/

Bond, C. (2022, August 5). *When And Why To Surrender A Life Insurance Policy.* Forbes Advisor. https://www.forbes.com/advisor/life-insurance/surrender-life-insurance-policy/

Bonds | Investor.gov. (n.d.). https://www.investor.gov/introduction-investing/investing-basics/investment-products/bonds-or-fixed-income-products/bonds

Boyd, C. (2021, August 26). *Plug Your Spending Leaks.* Molen & Associates. https://molentax.com/plug-your-spending-leaks/

Brown, K. (2022, September 8). *7 Steps For Transforming Your Relationship With Money.* Clever Girl Finance. https://www.clevergirlfinance.com/blog/transforming-your-relationship-with-money/

Build an Emergency Fund. (2022, June 30). Investopedia. https://www.investopedia.com/personal-finance/how-to-build-emergency-fund/

Butcher, S. (2022, October 7). *The Rich Get Richer & The Poor Get Poorer (+ Video).* Calmpreneur®. https://calmpreneur.com/rich-get-richer-eft-tapping/

Butsch, C. (2022, March 10). *7 reasons why you should have car insurance.* Money Under 30. https://www.moneyunder30.com/why-do-you-need-car-insurance

Can I Withdraw Money From My Universal Life Insurance Policy? (2020, September 2). Life Ant. https://www.lifeant.com/faq/can-i-withdraw-money-from-my-universal-life-insurance-policy/

Car Loans. (2022, May 9). Investopedia. https://www.investopedia.com/auto-loans-4689734

Cash vs. Credit: Which to Use? (n.d.). Capital One. https://www.capitalone.com/learn-grow/money-management/when-to-use-cash-vs-credit/

Castrillon, C. (2020, July 12). *5 Ways To Go From A Scarcity To Abundance Mindset.* Forbes. https://www.forbes.com/sites/carolinecastrillon/2020/07/12/5-ways-to-go-from-a-scarcity-to-abundance-mindset/?sh=77bebfa71197

Check: What It Is, How Bank Checks Work, and How To Write One. (2021, August 11). Investopedia. https://www.investopedia.com/terms/c/check.asp

CHN Financial Consultancy. (n.d.). *5 Benefits of Saving Money | CHN.* https://www.chnfc.co.uk/5-benefits-of-saving-money

Comai-Legrand, L. (2022, December 5). *Pros and Cons of Renting vs Buying a Home.* https://www.firstalliancecu.com/blog/pros-and-cons-of-renting-and-buying-a-home

Cooper, S. (2022, November 23). *A Look at IUL Fees, Costs, & Illustration Manipulation.* FIG Marketing. https://www.figmarketing.com/blog/a-look-at-iul-fees-costs-and-illustration-manipulation/

Correa, J. (2022, June 23). *How Do Car Loans Work?* Forbes Advisor. https://www.forbes.com/advisor/auto-loans/how-do-car-loans-work/

Creating a budget is one of the best financial decisions you can make for yourself and your family. Not only does a budget help you determine and reach your long-term goals, it will also help you manage your day-to-day spending and gain control over your finances. (n.d.). Blackhawk Bank. https://www.blackhawkbank.com/top-budgeting-myths

Credit Cards vs. Debit Cards: What's the Difference? (2023, March 2). Investopedia. https://www.investopedia.com/articles/personal-finance/050214/credit-vs-debit-cards-which-better.asp

Credit: What It Is and How It Works. (2023, February 14). Investopedia. https://www.investopedia.com/terms/c/credit.asp

Croll, M. (2022, November 2). *What is Universal Life Insurance? Pros and Cons.* ValuePenguin. https://www.valuepenguin.com/life-insurance/universal-life-insurance

Cruze, R. (2022, July 14). *A Quick Guide to Your Emergency Fund.* Ramsey Solutions. https://www.ramseysolutions.com/saving/quick-guide-to-your-emergency-fund

Cryptocurrency Explained With Pros and Cons for Investment. (2023, February 4). Investopedia. https://www.investopedia.com/terms/c/cryptocurrency.asp

Cryptocurrency Investing. (n.d.). Schwab Brokerage. https://www.schwab.com/cryptocurrency

D. (n.d.-). *Universal Life Insurance, Indexed Universal Life, Variable Life Insurance.* https://www.mutualofomaha.com/life-insurance/universal-life-insurance

Das, Y. (2022, November 9). *Know all about Insurance benefits & types.* A Comprehensive Guide to Money Transfer, Recharges, Bill Payments and Other Digital Payments | Paytm Blog. https://paytm.com/blog/insurance/what-is-insurance-definition-benefits-and-types/

Davis, C., & Taube, S. (2023, February 23). *How to Invest in Stocks.* NerdWallet. https://www.nerdwallet.com/article/investing/how-to-invest-in-stocks

Debt Management Guide. (2023, February 12). Investopedia. https://www.investopedia.com/articles/pf/12/good-debt-bad-debt.asp

Debt: What It Is, How It Works, Types, and Ways to Pay Back. (2023, February 28). Investopedia. https://www.investopedia.com/terms/d/debt.asp

Deferment and Forbearance | Trinity Debt Management. (n.d.). https://www.trinitycredit.org/deferment-and-forbearance

Defining Your Basic Investing Objectives: What To Factor In. (2022, May 21). Investopedia. https://www.investopedia.com/managing-wealth/basic-investment-objectives/

Dieker, N. (2023, February 27). *Why is good credit so important?* Bankrate. http://www.bankrate.com/personal-finance/credit/why-is-good-credit-so-important/

Do I Really Need Disability Insurance? (n.d.). MetLife. https://www.metlife.com/stories/accident-health/do-i-really-need-disability-insurance/

Effects of inflation on investments. (2022, September 16). https://www.usbank.com/financialiq/invest-your-money/investment-strategies/effects-of-inflation-on-investments.html

Episode #4: The Costs Associated with an Indexed Universal Life Policy. (n.d.). https://www.lifepro.com/Blog/PostId/1792/the-costs-associated-with-an-indexed-universal-life-policy

Episode #31: What Type of Return Can I Expect from My IUL Policy? (n.d.). https://www.lifepro.com/Blog/PostId/1827/what-type-of-return-can-i-expect-from-my-iul-policy

F. (2022b, July 8). *4 Reasons it's Important for Kids to Learn Financial Literacy.* FFCCU. https://www.ffcommunity.com/4-reasons-its-important-for-kids-to-learn-financial-literacy

Ferreira, N. M. (2023, January 19). *11 Best Side Hustle Ideas to Make an Extra ",000 a Month.* https://www.oberlo.com/blog/side-hustle

Financial psychologist explores attitudes toward money | Emory University | Atlanta GA. (n.d.). Emory University. https://news.emory.edu/stories/2017/07/er_financial_psychologist/campus.html

Firestone, E. S. A. \. C. C. (2020, October 12). *Side Hustle Ideas: How to Find Yours and Make an Extra ",000 A Month (And More).* Shopify. https://www.shopify.com/ph/blog/side-hustle

Following These 10 Steps Will Help Avoid Creating Credit Card Debt. (2022, January 17). The Balance. https://www.thebalancemoney.com/avoid-credit-card-debt-960043

Forbidden | Error | SmartAsset.com. (n.d.). https://smartasset.com/retirement/indexed-universal-life-insurance-iul

Free, F. C. O. (2021, August 7). *How To Save Money Fast With A Spending Freeze.* Fun Cheap or Free. https://funcheaporfree.com/how-to-do-a-spending-freeze/

Furniss, M. (n.d.). *Common causes of debt*. Norton Finance. https://www.nortonfinance.co.uk/know-how/debt-management/common-causes-of-debt

Galavan, K. (2021, January 8). *16 Budgeting Myths That Are Holding You Back*. Forever Break. https://foreverbreak.com/lifestyle/budgeting-myths/

George, D. (2023, February 22). *Indexed Universal Life (IUL) Insurance: What It Is and Whether It's for You*. The Motley Fool. https://www.fool.com/the-ascent/insurance/life/indexed-universal-life-insurance-iul/

Glantz, J. (2020, September 16). *I made 3 changes to my savings strategy after learning about compound interest, and now I'm earning more than ever*. Business Insider. https://www.businessinsider.com/personal-finance/earning-more-with-compound-interest-2020-9?international=true&r=US&IR=T

Glover, L., & Bradley, S. (2023, March 1). *How to Get a Car Loan*. NerdWallet. https://www.nerdwallet.com/article/loans/auto-loans/how-to-get-a-car-loan

Goldberg, M. (2022, September 12). *Banks vs. credit unions: How to decide where to keep your money*. Bankrate. https://www.bankrate.com/banking/banks-vs-credit-unions/

Gregory, R. (2021, July 26). *The Advantages And Disadvantages Of Taking Out A Loan*. https://www.wales247.co.uk/the-advantages-and-disadvantages-of-taking-out-a-loan

Gustafson, B. (2022, December 11). *Pros and Cons of Investing in a 401(k) Retirement Plan*. Triton Financial Group. http://tritonfinancialgroup.com/pros-cons-investing-401k-retirement-plan/

H. (2022, June 14). *Historical Market Movements and IUL*. Banking Truths. https://bankingtruths.com/videos/market-history-and-iul/

Hasenstab, M. (2022, August 30). *15 Ways to Plug Leaks in Your Budget*. https://www.stlouisfed.org/open-vault/2020/april/ways-plug-leaks-household-budget

Hazell, A. (n.d.). *Compound Interest Calculator*. The Calculator Site. https://www.thecalculatorsite.com/finance/calculators/compoundinterestcalculator.php

Helhoski, A. (2023, January 5). *Which to Borrow: Subsidized vs. Unsubsidized Student Loans*. NerdWallet. https://www.nerdwallet.com/article/loans/student-loans/unsubsidized-student-loans

Hi my name is (name) and I'm a shopaholic. (2021, September 29). Reddit. https://www.reddit.com/r/femalefashionadvice/comments/pxxedd/hi_my_name_is_name_and_im_a_shopaholic/

How Does Inflation Affect Your Finances. (n.d.). Pru Life UK. https://www.prulifeuk.com.ph/en/explore-pulse/health-financial-wellness/high-inflation-hurts-your-finances-more-than-you-think

How Fear, Guilt, Shame and Envy Affect Your Financial Goals. (n.d.). https://www.money254.co.ke/post/money-and-emotions-how-fear-guilt-shame-and-envy-affect-your-financial-goals

How To Choose A Credit Card. (n.d.). https://time.com/nextadvisor/credit-cards/how-to-choose-a-credit-card/

How to Consolidate Student Loans. (2022, November 24). Investopedia. https://www.investopedia.com/articles/personal-finance/011916/student-loan-refinancing-pros-and-cons.asp

How to Improve Your Credit Score Fast. (2022, November 4). Investopedia. https://www.investopedia.com/how-to-improve-your-credit-score-4590097

How to invest in bonds. (n.d.). BlackRock. https://www.blackrock.com/us/individual/education/how-to-invest-in-bonds

How to Invest in Cryptocurrency. (2022, September 24). Investopedia. https://www.investopedia.com/investing-in-cryptocurrency-5215269

How to Make a Zero Based Budget. (n.d.). https://www.ramseysolutions.com/budgeting/how-to-make-a-zero-based-budget#:~:text=Zero%2 Based%20budgeting%20 is%20 when,%2C%20a%20job%2C%20a%20 goal

How Variable Universal Life Insurance Works | Thrivent. (2023, January 23). Thrivent.com. https://www.thrivent.com/insights/life-insurance/how-variable-universal-life-insurance-works

How waiting 24 hours can avoid buyerâs remorse | Metrobank. (n.d.). https://www.metrobank.com.ph/articles/learn/how-to-avoid-buyers-remorse

Huffman, E. (2022, June 24). *Best Variable Life Insurance for February 2023* •. Benzinga. https://www.benzinga.com/money/best-variable-life-insurance

Hunt, J. (2023, February 16). *What Does It Mean to Set SMART Financial Goals? - CCS.* Credit Counselling Society. https://nomoredebts.org/blog/budgeting-saving/what-does-it-mean-to-set-smart-financial-goals

I think I'm a Shopaholic. (2022, February 17). Reddit.cubahttps://www.reddit.com/r/personalfinance/comments/susa7a/i_think_im_a_shopaholic/

Importance of Health Insurance and Why Do You Need It? (n.d.). https://www.hdfcbank.com/personal/resources/learning-centre/insure/importance-of-health-insurance-and-why-do-you-need-it

Importance of Savings - Know 5 Reasons to Save Money | ICICI Prulife. (n.d.). https://www.iciciprulife.com/protection-saving-plans/importance-of-savings.html

Improve or Rebuild Credit | Wells Fargo. (n.d.-). https://www.wellsfargo.com/goals-credit/smarter-credit/improve-credit/rebuild-credit/

Income Expenses Budget. (n.d.). https://www.canada.ca/en/financial-consumer-agency/services/financial-toolkit/income-expenses-budget/income-expenses-budget-3/6.html

Index Universal Life Insurance. (n.d.). Transamerica. https://www.transamerica.com/insurance/index-universal-life-insurance

Indexed Universal Life Insurance Buying Guide | Guardian. (n.d.). https://www.guardianlife.com/life-insurance/indexed-universal

Indexed Universal Life Insurance (IUL) Meaning and Pros and Cons. (2022, November 4). Investopedia. https://www.investopedia.com/articles/personal-finance/012416/pros-and-cons-indexed-universal-life-insurance.asp

Indexed Universal Life (IUL) Explained. (n.d.). Ogletree Financial. https://insurancequotes2day.com/indexed-universal-life-iul-explained/

Insurance: Definition, How It Works, and Main Types of Policies. (2022, July 19). Investopedia. https://www.investopedia.com/terms/i/insurance.asp

Interview With Consumer Affairs Expert Kathryn J. Morrison. (2022, May 9). Investopedia. https://www.investopedia.com/how-car-loans-work-5202265

Investing Explained: Types of Investments and How To Get Started. (2022, July 22). Investopedia. https://www.investopedia.com/terms/i/investing.asp

Investing in cryptocurrency. (2022, May 4). Investopedia. https://www.investopedia.com/cryptocurrency-4427699

Iversen, J. (2022, September 20). *How to use Indexed Universal Life [IUL] Insurance - WealthFit.* https://wealthfit.com. https://wealthfit.com/articles/iul-indexed-universal-life-insurance/

Jackson, T. (2023, February 16). *What You Need to Know This Tax Season (2022-23 Guide).* InCharge Debt Solutions. https://www.incharge.org/financial-literacy/budgeting-saving/how-to-cut-your-expenses/

James Royal. (2022a, July 15). *A complete guide to 401(k) retirement plans: What is a 401(k)?* Bankrate. https://www.bankrate.com/retirement/401k/

James Royal. (2022b, December 19). *How to invest in real estate in 2022.* Bankrate. https://www.bankrate.com/investing/how-to-invest-in-real-estate/

James Royal. (2023a, February 22). *How to start investing in cryptocurrency: A guide for beginners.* Bankrate. https://www.bankrate.com/investing/how-to-invest-in-cryptocurrency-beginners-guide/

James Royal. (2023b, February 22). *Stock market basics: 9 tips for beginners.* Bankrate. https://www.bankrate.com/investing/stock-market-basics-for-beginners/

John J. Beckley Quote. (n.d.). A-Z Quotes. https://www.azquotes.com/quote/710547

Just a moment. . . (n.d.-a). *Money Doesn't Buy Happiness.* http://moneytamer.com/money-doesnt-buy-happiness/

Just a moment. . . (n.d.-). *How to Mitigate Market Risk.* https://reciprocity.com/blog/how-to-mitigate-market-risk/

K. (2020, December 12). *How To Prepare For Your First Spending Freeze Challenge.* True Money Saver. https://truemoneysaver.com/no-spend/prepare-for-spending-freeze/

Kamel, G. (2023, February 3). *Indexed Universal Life Insurance (IUL), Explained.* Ramsey Solutions. https://www.ramseysolutions.com/insurance/indexed-universal-life-insurance

Kenkare, P. (2022, August 21). *Here's the Best Way to Start a Side Hustle and Make Extra Money Each Month.* CNET. https://www.cnet.com/personal-finance/heres-the-best-way-to-start-a-side-hustle-and-make-extra-money-each-month/

Key Benefits of Investing in Stocks. (n.d.). https://www6.royalbank.com/en/di/hubs/investing-academy/chapter/key-benefits-of-investing-in-stocks/jv7atg13/jv7atg1j

Kilroy, A. (2022, April 11). *Universal Life Insurance Explained.* Forbes Advisor. https://www.forbes.com/advisor/life-insurance/universal-life-insurance/

L. (2021, May 12). *Building Wealth vs. Making Money.* John Hope Bryant. https://johnhopebryant.com/2021/05/building-wealth-vs-making-money.html

Lake, R. (2021, June 21). *How To Create An Emergency Fund.* Forbes Advisor. https://www.forbes.com/advisor/banking/how-to-create-an-emergency-fund/

Lake, R. (2023, January 4). *What Is A High-Yield Savings Account?* Forbes Advisor. https://www.forbes.com/advisor/banking/savings/what-is-a-high-yield-savings-account/

Lane, R., & Helhoski, A. (2022, November 29). *Student Loan Deferment vs. Forbearance: Which Payment Pause is Better?* NerdWallet. https://www.nerdwallet.com/article/loans/student-loans/student-loan-deferment-forbearance

Lazar, A. (2023, January 31). *How to Set S.M.A.R.T. Financial Goals (With Examples).* FinMasters. https://finmasters.com/smart-financial-goals/

Leefeldt, E. (2022, November 11). *Sounding The Alarm On Indexed Universal Life Insurance (IUL).* Forbes Advisor. https://www.forbes.com/advisor/life-insurance/indexed-universal-life-insurance-problems/

Lighthouse Life Solutions, LLC. (2022, December 12). *How to Sell a Universal Life Insurance Policy for Cash.* Lighthouse Life. https://www.lighthouselife.com/blog/how-to-sell-a-universal-life-insurance-policy-for-cash/

Limiting Beliefs About Money. (n.d.). https://financeoverfifty.com/wp-content/uploads/2020/11/Limiting-beliefs-about-money.png

Loredo, A. (2023, February 6). *Never Compare Yourself to Others: 6 Reasons Why.* Clever Girl Finance. https://www.clevergirlfinance.com/blog/never-compare-yourself-to-others/

Lyons, R. (2023, February 23). *Pros and Cons of Real Estate Investing: A Comprehensive Overview.* Investor Junkie. https://investorjunkie.com/real-estate/pros-and-cons/

Marder, A., & Rose, G. (2023, January 12). *What is Universal Life Insurance? Pros, Cons and Cost.* NerdWallet. https://www.nerdwallet.com/article/insurance/universal-life-insurance

Marquit, M. (2023, January 23). *5 types of mortgage loans for homebuyers.* Bankrate. https://www.bankrate.com/mortgages/types-of-mortgages/

Martin, E. J. (2022, November 16). *How to get a mortgage.* Bankrate. https://www.bankrate.com/mortgages/how-to-get-a-mortgage/

Miller, D. (2022, April 27). *Why it's More Important Than Ever to Track Your Spending.* MintLife Blog. https://mint.intuit.com/blog/planning/why-its-more-important-than-ever-to-track-your-spending/

Money, W. W. (2021, August 23). *Using Your Values to Make the Best Money Decisions.* Women Who Money. https://womenwhomoney.com/values-money-decisions/

Mutual Funds | Investor.gov. (n.d.). https://www.investor.gov/introduction-investing/investing-basics/investment-products/mutual-funds-and-exchange-traded-1

Mutual Funds: Advantages and Disadvantages. (2021, December 1). Investopedia. https://www.investopedia.com/ask/answers/10/mutual-funds-advantages-disadvantages.asp

Mutual Funds: Different Types and How They Are Priced. (2022, June 28). Investopedia. https://www.investopedia.com/terms/m/mutualfund.asp

N. (2023, February 14). *Tracking Monthly Expenses: The First Step to Money Success.* NerdWallet. https://www.nerdwallet.com/article/finance/tracking-monthly-expenses

Napoletano, E. (2022, April 4). *What Is Investing? How Can You Start Investing?* Forbes Advisor. https://www.forbes.com/advisor/investing/what-is-investing/

Nbd, E. (n.d.). *How to avoid debt.* Emirates NBD. https://www.emiratesnbd.com/en/corporate-social-responsibility/financial-literacy/articles/how-to-avoid-debt/

New York Life. (2022, December 6). *Why Do I Need to Get Life Insurance?* https://www.newyorklife.com/articles/six-reasons-to-buy-life-insurance

Newth, M. (2022, June 14). *IUL's Fees Examined and Explained.* Banking Truths. https://bankingtruths.com/videos/iul-charges/

One more step. (n.d.). https://www.valleyfcu.com/about/blog/blog-detail.html?cId=59951

Opperman, M. (2022, July 22). *The Difference in Saving Money and Building Wealth.* Credit.org. https://credit.org/blog/the-difference-in-saving-money-and-building-wealth/

Opportunity Cost. (2020, January 28). Econlib. https://www.econlib.org/library/Topics/College/opportunitycost.html

O'Shea, A. (2022, November 16). *How to Invest in Real Estate: 5 Ways to Get Started.* NerdWallet. https://www.nerdwallet.com/article/investing/5-ways-to-invest-in-real-estate

O'Shea, B., & Schwahn, L. (2023, February 14). *6 Ways to Rebuild Credit.* NerdWallet. https://www.nerdwallet.com/article/finance/ways-to-rebuild-credit

Partida, D. (2022, July 4). *Selling Stuff as a Side Hustle.* Entrepreneur. https://www.entrepreneur.com/business-news/selling-stuff-as-a-side-hustle/430747

Pay Yourself First: Learn Why | Wells Fargo. (n.d.). https://www.wellsfargo.com/financial-education/basic-finances/manage-money/cashflow-savings/pay-yourself-first/

Payment types. (n.d.). https://tfig.unece.org/contents/payments-types.htm

Payne, K. (2022, July 13). *Why you should have money conversations with your children early.* Bankrate. https://www.bankrate.com/finance/credit-cards/ways-to-teach-kids-financial-literacy-early/

Perez, K. (2021, August 18). *Do You Have Good Money Values?* Chime. https://www.chime.com/blog/do-you-have-good-money-values/

Plummer, S. (2022, July 27). *How To Cash Out A Life Insurance Policy Before Death? (2023).* The Annuity Expert. https://www.annuityexpertadvice.com/cash-out-life-insurance-policy-before-death/

PMI: Costs of Private Mortgage Insurance and How to Avoid Them. (2022, March 23). Investopedia. https://www.investopedia.com/ask/answers/09/pmi.asp

Policygenius. (n.d.). https://www.policygenius.com/life-insurance/how-to-cancel-your-life-insurance-policy/

Porter, K. (2022, November 17). *Deferment vs. forbearance: Which is best for your student loan?* Bankrate. http://www.bankrate.com/loans/student-loans/deferment-or-forbearance-student-loans/

Promotional Feature, HT Brand Studio. (2018, February 5). *Money myths: 5 stereotypes about women and finances that we need to bust right now | Mint.* Mint. https://www.livemint.com/Home-Page/LGiSxKK2Q2mZfiBXjCnVJP/Money-myths-5-stereotypes-about-women-and-finances-that-we.html

Pros and Cons of Indexed Universal Life Insurance. (2022, November 22). Investopedia. https://www.investopedia.com/articles/personal-finance/070215/pros-cons-indexed-universal-life-insurance.asp

Pros and Cons of Leasing or Buying a Car. (2023, February 9). Investopedia. https://www.investopedia.com/articles/personal-finance/012715/when-leasing-car-better-buying.asp

Pros and Cons of Managing Your 401(k) Yourself. (2021, March 16). Investopedia. https://www.investopedia.com/articles/personal-finance/032616/managing-your-own-401k-pros-cons.asp

Pros and Cons of Student Loan Consolidation for Federal Loans. (2022, August 30). Debt.org. https://www.debt.org/students/pros-and-cons-of-student-loan-consolidation/

Ramsey Solutions. (2022, December 15). *How the Debt Snowball Method Works.* https://www.ramseysolutions.com/debt/how-the-debt-snowball-method-works

Registered Indexed Universal Life. (n.d.). https://us.milliman.com/-/media/milliman/pdfs/articles/registered-indexed-universal-life-concept-paper.ashx

Renting vs. Buying a Home: What's the Difference? (2022, July 31). Investopedia. https://www.investopedia.com/articles/personal-finance/083115/renting-vs-owning-home-pros-and-cons.asp

Richards, C. (2016, August 10). *One Secret to Cutting Spending: Wait 72 Hours Before You Buy.* The New York Times. https://www.nytimes.com/2016/08/10/your-money/one-secret-to-cutting-spending-wait-72-hours-before-you-buy.html

ROBBINS RESEARCH INTERNATIONAL, INC. (2021, May 27). *What is delayed gratification and why is it so important in life?* tonyrobbins.com. https://www.tonyrobbins.com/achieve-lasting-weight-loss/delayed-gratification

Robertson, C. (2021, August 20). *Renting vs. Buying a Home: 55 Pros and Cons.* The Truth About Mortgage. https://www.thetruthaboutmortgage.com/renting-vs-buying-55-pros-and-cons/

S. (n.d.-). *How Do Limiting Beliefs Harm Us? Here Are 5 Ways.* Finance Over Fifty. https://financeoverfifty.com/the-high-cost-of-limiting-beliefs/

S. (2022, April 28). *Money Values: How To Align Your Priorities With Your Spending.* Finance Over Fifty. https://financeoverfifty.com/money-values/

Schnaubelt, C. (2019, February 15). *The Pros And Cons Of Credit Cards.* Forbes. https://www.forbes.com/sites/catherineschnaubelt/2019/02/15/the-pros-and-cons-of-credit-cards/?sh=76eb635c1e8b

Schneider, J. (2023, February 14). *Is IUL a Scam? Yes.* Personal Finance Club. https://www.personalfinanceclub.com/is-iul-a-scam-yes/

Schwahn, L. (2023, February 27). *Financial Goals: Definition and Examples.* NerdWallet. https://www.nerdwallet.com/article/finance/financial-goals-definition-examples

Scott, S. (2022, September 23). *What You Need to Know About Universal Life Insurance Pros and Cons.* Healthmarkets Agents/Content/Plans. https://www.healthmarkets.com/resources/life-insurance/look-universal-life-insurance-pros-cons/

Securian Financial. (n.d.). *5 steps to build an emergency fund.* https://www.securian.com/insights-tools/articles/5-steps-to-building-an-emergency-fund.html

SelfMadeLadies Manifestation Blog by Mia Fox. (2022, August 13). *13 Most Common Limiting Beliefs About Money.* SelfMadeLadies. https://selfmadeladies.com/money-beliefs-limit-abundance/

Shubel, M. (2022, September 1). *How To Overcome Your Limiting Beliefs About Money.* Clever Girl Finance. https://www.clevergirlfinance.com/blog/limiting-beliefs-about-money/

Six Key Steps to Setting up an IUL the Better Money Method Way | The Better Money Method. (2018, March 5). https://www.bettermoneymethod.com/six-key-steps-creating-iul-policy-works/

Sorrentino, F. (2022, September 26). *Banking For All Generations.* Forbes. https://www.forbes.com/sites/franksorrentino/2022/09/26/banking-for-all-generations/?sh=46c8eecb45a0

Spann, S. (2018, January 14). *Are Your Money Beliefs Holding You Back?* Forbes. https://www.forbes.com/sites/financialfinesse/2018/01/14/are-your-money-beliefs-holding-you-back/?sh=1ad59e7079bd

Stocks | Investor.gov. (n.d.). https://www.investor.gov/introduction-investing/investing-basics/investment-products/stocks

Strategies to Mitigate Volatility. (n.d.). https://www.agf.com/us/building-resilient-portfolios/mitigate-risk/index.jsp

Student Loan Debt: 2022 Statistics and Outlook. (2023, February 27). Investopedia. https://www.investopedia.com/student-loan-debt-2019-statistics-and-outlook-4772007

Student Loan Forbearance: Pros and Cons. (2022, November 29). Investopedia. https://www.investopedia.com/student-loan-forbearance-pros-and-cons-4771305

Student Loan Repayment Options: What's the Best Way to Pay? (2022a, December 2). Investopedia. https://www.investopedia.com/student-loan-repayment-options-what-s-the-best-way-to-pay-4772402

Student Loan Repayment Options: What's the Best Way to Pay? (2022b, December 2). Investopedia. https://www.investopedia.com/student-loan-repayment-options-what-s-the-best-way-to-pay-4772402

Stueber, S. (2021, October 19). *Eight tips for choosing the right insurance company.* https://www.thesilverlining.com/westbendcares/blog/eight-tips-for-choosing-the-right-insurance-company

Subsidized vs. Unsubsidized Student Loans: Which Is Best? (2023, February 27). Investopedia. https://www.investopedia.com/personal-finance/federal-direct-loans-subsidized-vs-unsubsidized/

Suknanan, J. (2023, January 31). *What is a mortgage and how does it work?* CNBC. https://www.cnbc.com/select/what-is-a-mortgage-and-how-does-it-work/

Surviving Tough Times by Building Resilience. (n.d.). HelpGuide.org. https://www.helpguide.org/articles/stress/surviving-tough-times.htm

Swoboda, K. (2022, January 27). *The fear of not having enough money.* Kate Swoboda. http://www.yourcourageouslife.com/blog/fear-of-not-having-enough-money

The 3 Things That Create Your Money Beliefs. (n.d.). https://www.healthyloveandmoney.com/blog/the-3-things-that-create-your-money-beliefs

The Difference Between Wants and Needs. (2022, June 20). The Balance. https://www.thebalancemoney.com/how-to-separate-wants-and-needs-453592

The Importance of Property Insurance. (2021, September 7). Investopedia. https://www.investopedia.com/articles/insurance/09/property-insurance.asp

The Power of Compound Interest: Calculations and Examples. (2022, July 19). Investopedia. https://www.investopedia.com/terms/c/compoundinterest.asp

The Side Effects of Bad Credit. (2021, June 11). Investopedia. https://www.investopedia.com/the-side-effects-of-bad-credit-4769783

Three Factors to Consider When Choosing a Bank. (2022, April 29). Investopedia. https://www.investopedia.com/how-to-choose-a-bank-5183999

Top 10 Best Indexed Universal Life (IUL) Insurance Companies. (2023, January 26). https://www.insuranceandestates.com/indexed-universal-life-iul-insurance/

Town, P. (2022, November 22). *7 Tips For Spending Money Wisely.* Rule #1 Investing. https://www.ruleoneinvesting.com/blog/financial-control/spending-money-wisely/

Understand Your Relationship with Money. (n.d.). Wespath Benefits & Investments. https://www.wespath.org//health-well-being/health-well-being-resources/financial-well-being/understand-your-relationship-with-money

Understanding Budgeting & Personal Finance. (2021, November 28). The Balance. https://www.thebalancemoney.com/personal-finance-budget-4802696

Understanding Mortgages. (n.d.). https://www.practicalmoneyskills.com/learn/life_events/buying_a_home/understanding_mortgages

Understanding Types of Credit. (n.d.). https://time.com/nextadvisor/credit-cards/understanding-types-of-credit/

Underwood, J. (2022, September 22). *Cash Vs. Credit: Which Should I Use?* Forbes Advisor. https://www.forbes.com/advisor/credit-cards/cash-vs-credit-which-should-i-use/

Van Haaften, E. (2023, February 9). *Life Insurance Policy Loans.* Affordable Life USA. https://affordablelifeusa.com/life-insurance-policy-loans/

VanSomeren, L. (2021a, March 26). *16 Types of Loans to Help You Make Necessary Purchases.* Forbes Advisor. https://www.forbes.com/advisor/loans/types-of-loans/

VanSomeren, L. (2021b, July 21). *9 Benefits Of Good Credit And How It Can Help You Financially.* Forbes Advisor. https://www.forbes.com/advisor/credit-score/benefits-of-good-credit/

Variable Life Insurance. (2022, December 13). Investopedia. https://www.investopedia.com/ask/answers/08/variable-life-insurance.asp

Variable Universal Life (VUL) Insurance: What It Is, How It Works. (2022, June 14). Investopedia. https://www.investopedia.com/terms/v/variableuniversallife.asp

Waterworth, K. (2022, September 21). *How to Start Investing in Real Estate: The Basics.* The Motley Fool. https://www.fool.com/investing/stock-market/market-sectors/real-estate-investing/basics/

Welcome. (n.d.-). https://www.sofi.com/learn/content/spend-wisely-while-still-budgeting/

Western & Southern Financial Group. (2022, April 26). *The Impact of Inflation on Your Savings & Investments.* https://www.westernsouthern.com/learn/financial-education/the-impact-of-inflation-on-your-savings-and-investments

What Are Surrender Charges? Definition, How They Work and Example. (2022, July 18). Investopedia. https://www.investopedia.com/terms/s/surrender-charge.asp

What Does Paying Yourself First Mean? How It Works and Goal. (2021, April 25). Investopedia. https://www.investopedia.com/terms/p/payyourselffirst.asp

What Is a 401(k) and How Does It Work? (2023, February 21). Investopedia. https://www.investopedia.com/terms/1/401kplan.asp

What Is a Budget? Plus 10 Budgeting Myths Holding You Back. (2022, May 28). Investopedia. https://www.investopedia.com/terms/b/budget.asp

What Is a High-Yield Savings Account? (2021, November 3). Investopedia. https://www.investopedia.com/articles/pf/09/high-yield-savings-account.asp

What Is a Loan, How Does It Work, Types, and Tips on Getting One. (2021, April 19). Investopedia. https://www.investopedia.com/terms/l/loan.asp

What Is a Mortgage? Types, How They Work, and Examples. (2022, November 4). Investopedia. https://www.investopedia.com/terms/m/mortgage.asp

What is Budgeting and Why is it Important? (n.d.). My Money Coach. http://www.mymoneycoach.ca/budgeting/what-is-a-budget-planning-forecasting

What is Credit and Why is It Important? - Great Lakes. (n.d.). My Great Lakes. http://mygreatlakes.org/educate/knowledge-center/credit.html

What Is Indexed Universal Life Insurance (IUL)? (2023, February 22). Investopedia. https://www.investopedia.com/articles/insurance/09/indexed-universal-life-insurance.asp

What Is Inflation and How Does Inflation Affect Investments? (2022, September 7). Investopedia. https://www.investopedia.com/ask/answers/what-is-inflation-and-how-should-it-affect-investing/

What is Insurance? Why is it Important? (n.d.). https://www.grangeinsurance.com/tips/what-is-insurance-why-is-it-important

What is Saving? (n.d.). https://bcra.gob.ar/BCRAyVos/Aprendiendo-a-ahorrar-que-es-el-ahorro-i.asp

What Is Universal Life Insurance? (n.d.). https://www.davidraefp.com/What-Is-Universal-Life-Insurance.c43.htm

What to know about the debt snowball vs avalanche method — Wells Fargo. (n.d.). https://www.wellsfargo.com/goals-credit/smarter-credit/manage-your-debt/snowball-vs-avalanche-paydown/

What's the Difference Between Good Debt and Bad Debt? (2021, November 27). The Balance. https://www.thebalancemoney.com/good-debt-vs-bad-debt-960029

When Should You Get Life Insurance? (2023, February 23). Investopedia. https://www.investopedia.com/articles/investing/072816/what-best-age-get-life-insurance.asp

White, A. (2023, January 23). *Secured credit cards vs. unsecured credit cards*. CNBC. https://www.cnbc.com/select/secured-credit-cards-vs-unsecured-credit-cards/

Why get Health Insurance Coverage if you are under 30. (n.d.). HealthCare.gov. https://www.healthcare.gov/young-adults/ready-to-apply/

Why Is It Important To Have Home Insurance? | RAC. (n.d.). https://www.rac.co.uk/insurance/home-insurance/guides/why-is-it-important-to-have-home-insurance

Women and Money: Challenging the Myths. (n.d.). Board of Governors of the Federal Reserve System. https://www.federalreserve.gov/newsevents/speech/duke20100501a.htm

Yale, A. J. (2023, January 20). *What to know about the scarcity mindset and how it affects women and their finances — and 6 ways to avoid it*. Business Insider. https://www.businessinsider.com/personal-finance/scarcity-mindset?international=true&r=US&IR=T

Yochim, D. (2023, February 23). *What Is a 401(k) Plan?* NerdWallet. https://www.nerdwallet.com/article/investing/what-is-a-401k

Zinn, D. (2022, August 8). *How to use the debt avalanche payment strategy*. Bankrate. https://www.bankrate.com/personal-finance/debt/debt-avalanche-method/

DASNEVES DEPINA
BIOGRAPHY

Hello, my name is Dasneves Depina. Born July 28, 1972, in a small town named Ribeira Da Barca on the island of Santiago, Cape Verde. I am the 10th child of Juvito Gomes Oliveira and Adelina Da Rosa Goncalves. In 1988, Cuba offered Cape Verde school district scholarships to selected students, and by my grades being of excellent merit, I was one of the chosen students to receive one. At fourteen, I had an opportunity to leave Cape Verde and go to Cuba for a better future. I decided to leave Cape Verde to pursue a higher education in Cuba. In 1994, I returned to Cape Verde with a certification in Health Statics and worked for fourteen years in the local hospital in Praia. In 2008, I moved to Boston and was in a relationship that did not work out, but I have a beautiful daughter. I'm married to Lucas Depina, with two beautiful children, ages 14 and 12. Now I am pursuing a career as an author.